Pesky Plants

by Thor Kommedahl

Published by the Ag Program Area
Minnesota Extension Service
University of Minnesota

Thor Kommedahl is a professor, Department of Plant Pathology, University of Minnesota. The section on mushrooms was contributed by Clyde M. Christensen, professor, Department of Plant Pathology. Diane Peltz, Agricultural Publications, was the creative director and coordinator; Michael Ruetten was the layout and graphic designer.

The original drawings were prepared under WPA (Works Progress Administration) Project 1630 (OP 165-1-71-124) in 1935-36 by the following artists working under the direction of professor Larson, professor of Agricultural Botany at the University of Minnesota, St. Paul: Arndt, Colby, Douglas, Gies, Kuban, Larents, Lindeman, McNeill and Zoller. The majority of the illustrations are by Lindeman.

Contents   Page

Pesky Plants

Nature has many pesky plants. Some cause skin irritations, some are poisonous when eaten, some cause injury because they have thorny fruits, leaves, or stems, some cause hayfever, and some are merely troublesome at beaches and on lakeshore property.

You're likely to encounter pesky plants everywhere: at home, summer resorts, campgrounds, parks, woods, fields, and playgrounds. PESKY PLANTS provides information on the identification, growth habits, and control measures of these annoying plants.

Poison Ivy

Irritating or Blister-Producing Plants

Poison Ivy

Poison ivy (*Toxicodendron radicans*) and sumacs reduce land values at summer resort areas and cause much suffering at summer camps, parks, beaches, and woodlands.

The poison found in this woody perennial is urushiol (actually four poisons that differ in minor chemical ways). It is found in the resin ducts of roots and stems and in leaves, flowers, and fruits. Pollen and leaf hairs are not poisonous. This means you will not be affected by poison ivy just from breezes blowing over the plant to you.

Poison ivy varies in growth habit from dwarf and erect forms to strangling or climbing forms that produce aerial rootlets that anchor the vines to fences, walls, or trees. Slender, creeping rootstocks grow from the bases of the stems and run underground for several yards; short leafy stems emerge from the soil from such rootstocks.

The leaves are alternate on the stem and are divided into three leaflets; each is oval shaped, pointed at the tip, and tapered to the base. The terminal leaflet is longer stalked than the two lateral ones. The leaf surface may be glossy, or dull green and smooth, or somewhat hairy. The leaf margin may vary from entire, to toothed, or somewhat lobed. In deep shade or in dry weather, leaves may be light green, yellowish green, or even red. In autumn, leaves turn yellow and bright red before falling.

3

The greenish-yellow flowers, borne in compact clusters, often pass unnoticed. The grayish-white, berry-like fruit measures up to about 1/4 inch in diameter and contains a one-seeded pit. Stripes on the fruit make it look like the segments of a peeled orange. Fruits persist on the shrub through the winter and are eaten by as many as 55 different species of birds in the United States. In this way, seeds can be dispersed from place to place. Because some plants produce only male flowers, fruits are not always found on a given plant.

Though often found in rich woods, poison ivy also thrives in pastures, fence rows, banks, waste places, and in dry, rocky fields throughout the North Central Region.

Don't mistake Virginia creeper or moonseed for poison ivy. Virginia creeper has five leaflets and moonseed is only three lobed. Hog peanut, although it has three leaflets, has pink or white flowers, produces a pod, and is a twining vine. Poison oak (*T. toxicarium*) which also has three leaflets, occurs in the southern part of the region, especially southern Iowa, Missouri, and Kansas.

Contact with broken or scarified (but not intact parts of) poison ivy causes inflammation and sometimes swelling of the skin. This may be followed by intense irritation and blisters. The blisters may break, releasing a liquid, but the liquid cannot cause more blisters. Eventually scabs or crusts form.

Some persons are more susceptible than others and may even be more susceptible at one time than at another. Moreover, the amount and availability of poison on the plant may vary somewhat from time to time. Initially, a person may be immune but with repeated exposure becomes sensitized. One may contact symptoms of poison ivy by handling clothing, or shoes, or even by petting animals that have been in contact with poison ivy.

The reaction of the poison with the skin is nearly instantaneous, which means that washing the affected area with strong soaps will only remove excess poison. But it's still a good idea to wash the affected area, since the excess poison may otherwise be transferred to unexposed parts of the skin. Washing with soap must be thorough, otherwise soap can remove natural skin oils and enable greater penetration by the toxin. Symptoms may appear in a few hours or a few days, but they usually are noticeable within 24 hours. For treatment, consult a physician. Washing with strong soap is not a treatment; it only removes excess poison. Nonprescription hydrocortisone creams or lotions may reduce irritation. ACTH or a cortisone derivative may

4

be administered by a physician in severe cases. Under no circumstances should you eat a leaf in the mistaken notion that this will promote immunity—severe gastric irritation and even death can result.

In large infestations, poison ivy can be controlled by mowing close to the ground in midsummer, followed by plowing and harrowing or by grazing sheep or goats. For smaller patches, the roots may be grubbed out. If poison ivy is grubbed out and burned, be careful not to stand in the smoke, as the oil will stick to particles of soot and be carried to the skin, causing severe irritation.

Some herbicides have given excellent control when applied in the full leaf stage in June and July. If desirable plants that might be injured by drift of sprays are close by, you can apply herbicides at the bases of poison ivy plants.

Poison Sumac

This baneful bog bush, known also as swamp sumac, poison dogwood, poison elder, poison ash, or thunderwood, can be more poisonous than its near relative, poison ivy. The conditions of poisoning and the toxic principles are the same as for poison ivy.

Poison sumac (*Toxicodendron vernix*), with greenish-white berries, can be distinguished from the harmless staghorn sumac and smooth sumac, which have red berries. Some confuse green ash with poison sumac. But green ash has only one stem per plant and the leaf margin is toothed, whereas poison sumac produces a clump of stems and has leaves with unbroken leaf margins.

The greenish-yellow flowers may be male or female and are arranged in a spreading or pendulous branch arising from the attachment point of leaf to stem. Flowers appear from May through July and the globular fruits ripen from August through November and are conspicuous all winter.

Poison sumac is a coarse shrub 6-20 feet tall that has smooth, gray bark and smooth branches. Plants have 7-13 leaflets per leaf and the leaves are opposite. The autumn foliage is orange to scarlet.

Poison sumacs are most common in the wet places, in bogs and swamps, where tamaracks grow or along streams and ditches, especially in southern parts of Michigan, Wisconsin and Minnesota. In contrast, the harmless sumacs grow only in well drained soil or even in fairly dry soils.

Because poison sumac is very poisonous, it is best to eradicate it with chemicals. Also, it may be safest to apply chemicals when the

Poison Sumac

plants are dormant. Certain mixtures or a soil sterilant can be applied to the bases of the shrubs with success. Some herbicides can be sprayed on the aerial parts of the shrubs in full leaf stage. The herbicide is then carried in the sap to the roots and kills the plants.

Spurges

Plants in this group of about 1600 species contain a highly acrid milky juice in stems, leaves, and roots. This juice may produce severe irritation and blistering of the skin. Most cases of poisoning result from snow-on-the-mountain. Spurges are found throughout the United States.

Snow-on-the-mountain (*Euphorbia marginata*) is a native annual often planted in gardens because the leaf margins are white and petal like. The simple leaves are alternate on the lower stem but are opposite—or whorled—on the upper part of the stem. The flowers are borne in clusters with three-forked branches. The fruit, a three-part capsule, is somewhat hairy as shown in the drawing. There are three seeds per capsule.

Cypress spurge (*Euphorbia cyparissias*), sometimes named graveyard spurge because of its frequent appearance in cemeteries, is a perennial herb. It was introduced into the United States from Europe, where it was grown as an ornamental. It frequently inhabits dry, gravelly, or sandy soils.

This weedy plant sometimes grows in densely tufted masses from a network of ropelike rootstocks, or clustered from buds at the crown of the plant, or even scattered from buds on the creeping roots. The stems are smooth, and the leaves are alternate but more thickly set on the stem than other spurges. Seeds are not common and reproduction occurs primarily by creeping roots and rootstocks.

Flowering spurge (*Euphorbia corollata*), known also as poison milkweed, is a native perennial that reproduces by seeds and rootstocks and is common in dry, sandy areas. The erect stems are simple—or only sparingly branched—smooth, and are about 3 feet tall. The flax-like leaves are alternate at the lower parts of the stem and opposite above. There may be 25-75 or more leaves along the stem. The showy, flower-like parts of the plant are not flowers at all, but are petal-like appendages below the flower.

Leafy spurge (*Euphorbia esula*) is a noxious perennial herb that reputedly made its way into southwestern Minnesota in oats brought from Russia in 1890.

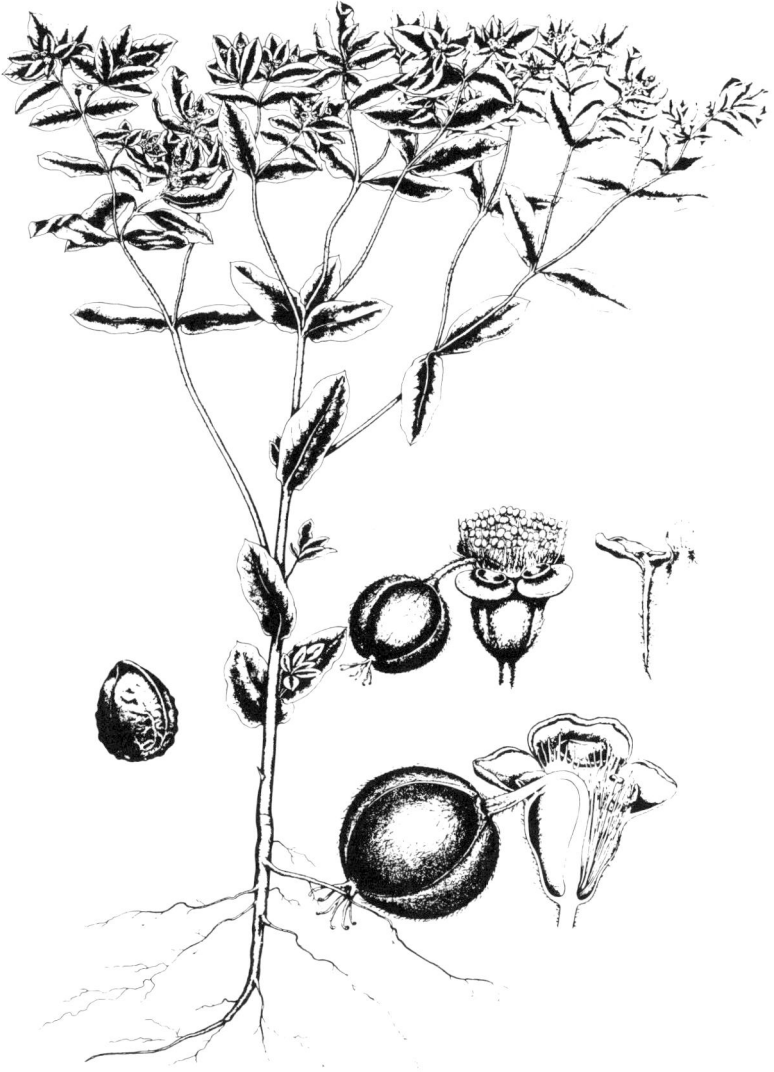

Snow-on-the-Mountain

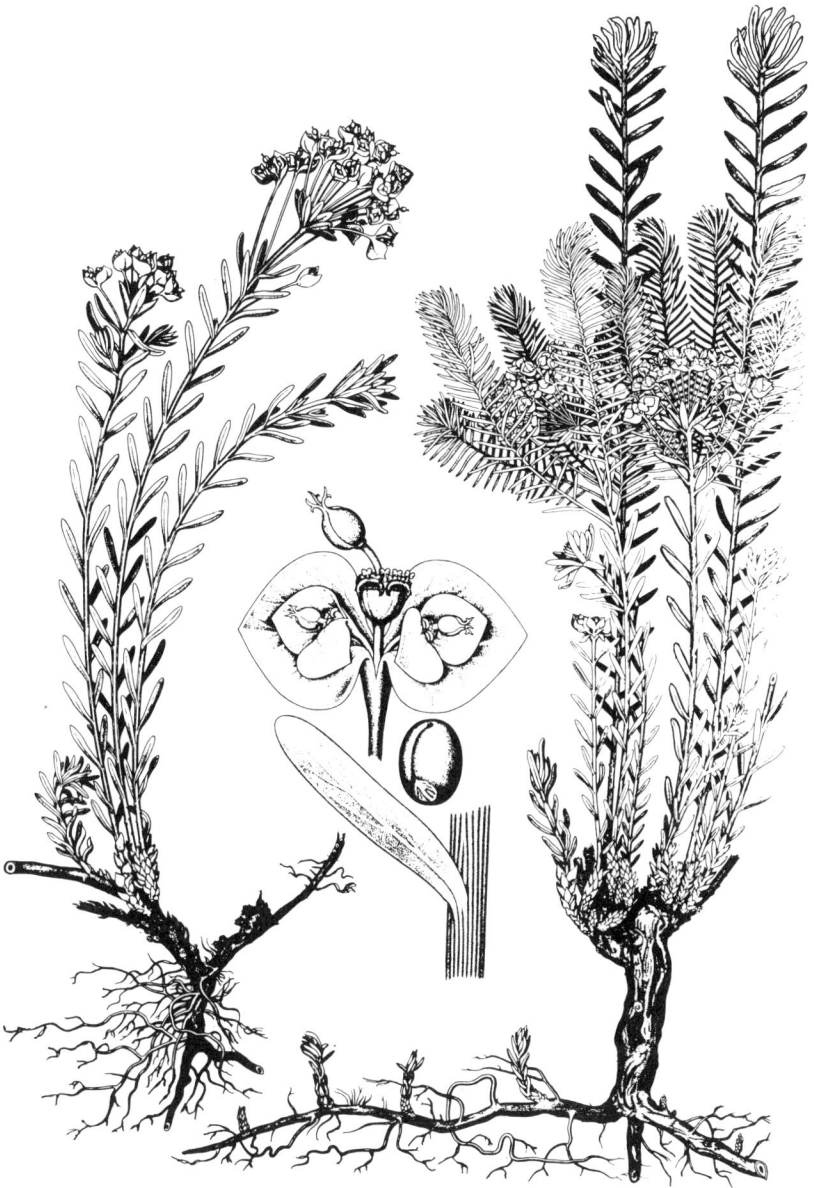

Cypress Spurge

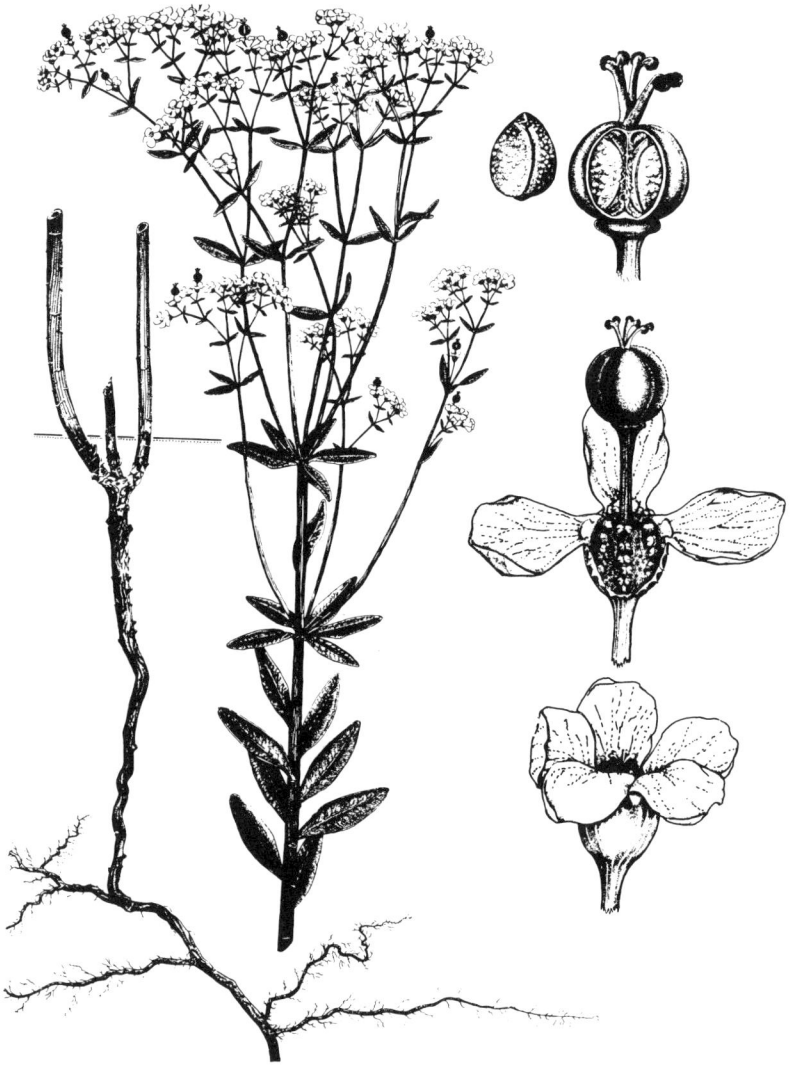

Flowering Spurge

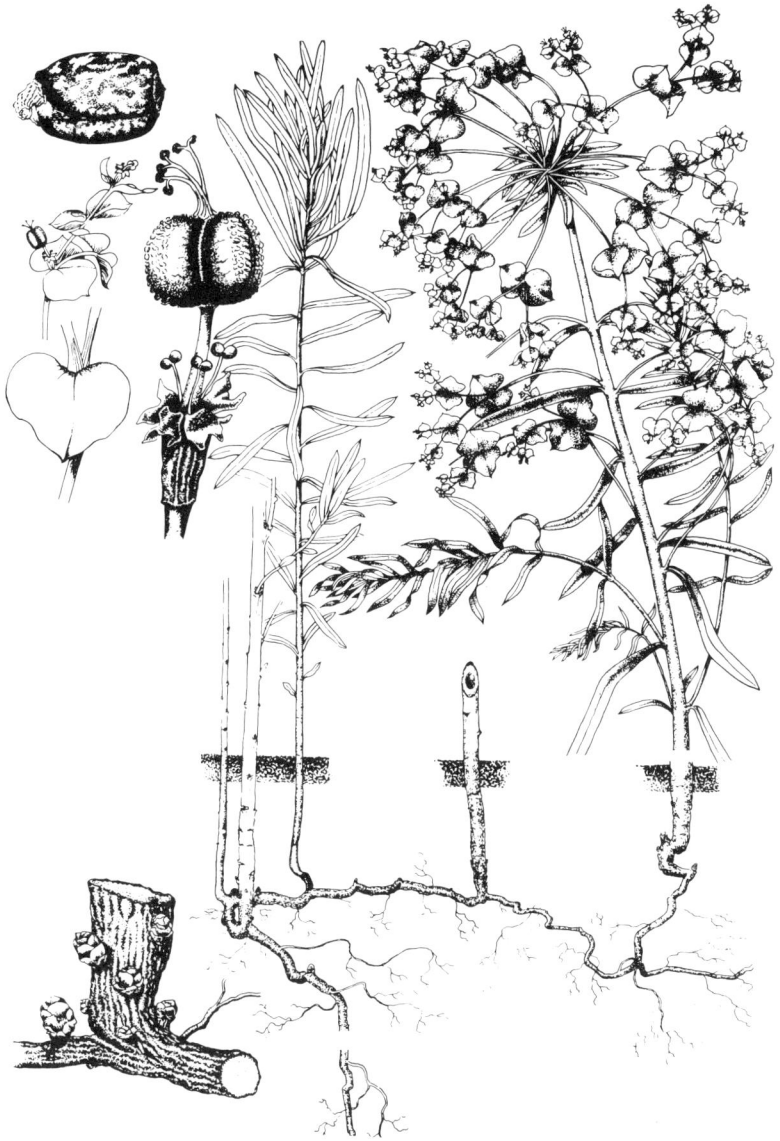

Leafy Spurge

11

It is deeply rooted; some roots grow 16 feet deep. The roots near the surface are creeping and aid in spreading the weed. The stem is erect and is simple—or branched—near the summit. Stems frequently are clustered from buds arising on the vertical root. In late summer, pinkish, scaly buds are visible just below the crown. The bluish-green leaves frequently turn to a brownish-orange toward autumn. Cuplike structures at the top of the plant contain the greenish-yellow flowers and at maturity a fruit (capsule) is formed which bursts and scatters seed. Some plants produce two or more crops of seed stalks per season.

If eaten, spurges are emetic and purgative. Also, there is swelling about the eyes and mouth, accompanied by abdominal pain. Purgatives sometimes are made from the cypress spurge and can be poisonous if taken in excess.

The spurges can be controlled by digging scattered plants if the infestation is small. Continuous mowing will prevent seed formation and exhaust food reserves in roots or underground stems.

It is difficult to kill spurges with herbicides. A combination of frequent mowing and repeated application of some herbicides is fairly effective. Small patches in noncrop areas can be eradicated with soil sterilants.

Nettles

There are two principal kinds of stinging nettles. One is wood nettle (*Laportea canadensis*), which grows mostly in rich, moist woods in deep shade or in the shade along streams or lakes. The other is the stinging nettle (*Urtica dioica*), which is common on higher ground, often growing in full sunlight. The stinging nettle is a perennial plant introduced from Eurasia and generally found in dense patches.

The wood nettle is a perennial plant native to the Americas. It often grows in dense stands in heavily shaded, moist woodlands. This nettle produces itching similar to that caused by stinging nettles.

The root system of both kinds of nettles is similar. An outstanding difference between nettles is the leaf arrangement. The wood nettle has alternate leaves and the stinging nettle opposite ones. Also, the leaves of wood nettle often are heart shaped.

Nettles generally are not poisonous, but they are irritating. The leaves usually are covered with hairs that have broad bases but taper toward the tip. At the slightest touch, the globular tip is knocked off,

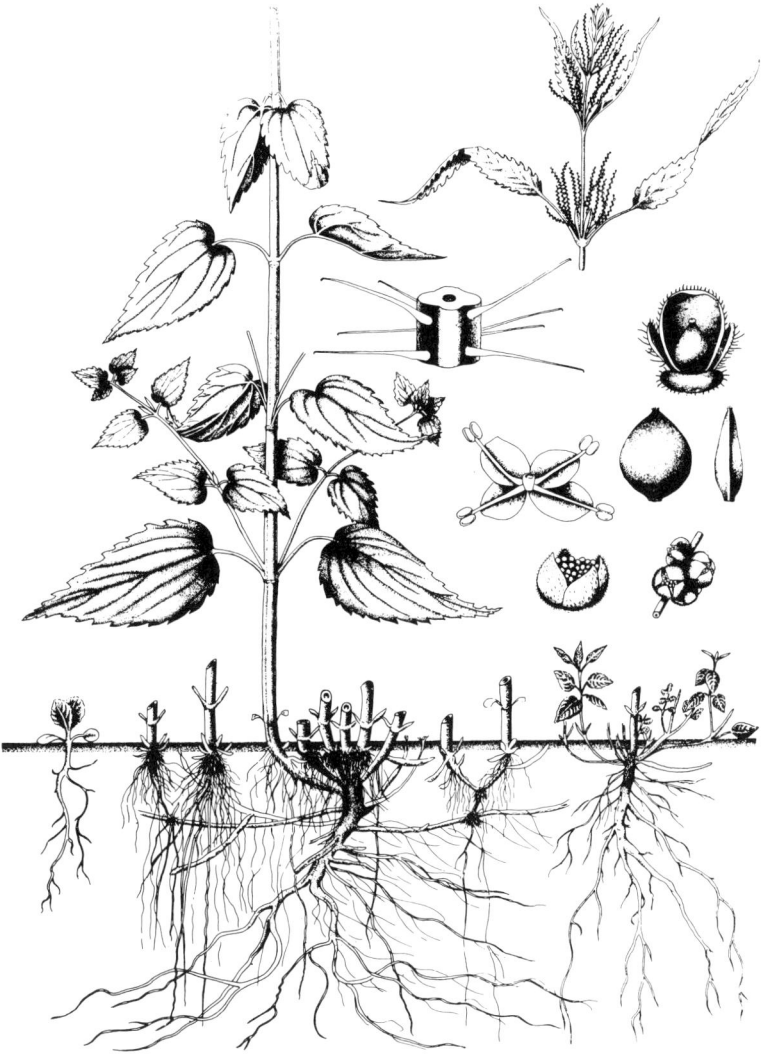

Stinging Nettle

13

leaving a sharp point that easily penetrates the skin. At the same time, a poisonous liquid consisting of acetylcholine, histamine, and 5-hydroxytryptamine oozes out of the hair into the skin, causing a burning sensation of short duration.

Many species of stinging nettles differ from the one just described in minor characteristics only. Stinging nettle has a strongly developed root system and a network of underground creeping rootstocks. The bristly, fibrous stems usually are four angled, but sometimes are irregularly angled with deep furrows in them. They contain a watery juice. The whole plant is covered with short bristles and long, stinging hairs. The coarsely toothed leaves are arranged opposite each other on the stem. There is a distinct middle vein in the leaf with branches on the leaf margin. The flowers are small, greenish, without petals, and are borne on the stem just above the point where the leaves are attached. The seeds are flat, granular, and about the size of a pinhead.

Nettles can be controlled by grubbing out the rootstocks and killing by drying, if this is feasible. Mowing frequently and close to the ground will prevent seed formation as well as exhaust food reserves stored in the roots and rootstocks. Nettles also can be killed by spraying them with herbicides.

Smartweeds

There are many species of smartweeds (46 species in northeastern North America). Many of these contain juices that are bitterly pungent or peppery and cause smarting or irritation to the eyes and nostrils. People who are sensitive to smartweeds occasionally develop skin rashes, or develop a sensitivity to sunlight.

The common smartweed (*Polygonum hydropiper*) probably is the most irritating of the smartweeds. It is weak stemmed and is found primarily in damp or wet places. The stems are reddish and have swollen joints. There is a papery sheath just above each joint. The leaves are alternate and shaped like willow leaves. The greenish flowers produce purplish-black seeds that may be flattened or somewhat three-angled.

Ladysthumb smartweed (*Polygonum persicaria*) differs from common smartweed in that it has a somewhat triangular purple blotch on each leaf, which gives the species its name. Weak stems, willow-shaped leaves, and swollen joints also are characteristic of this species. The flowers are pink or rose colored. The flattened or triangular

Common Smartweed

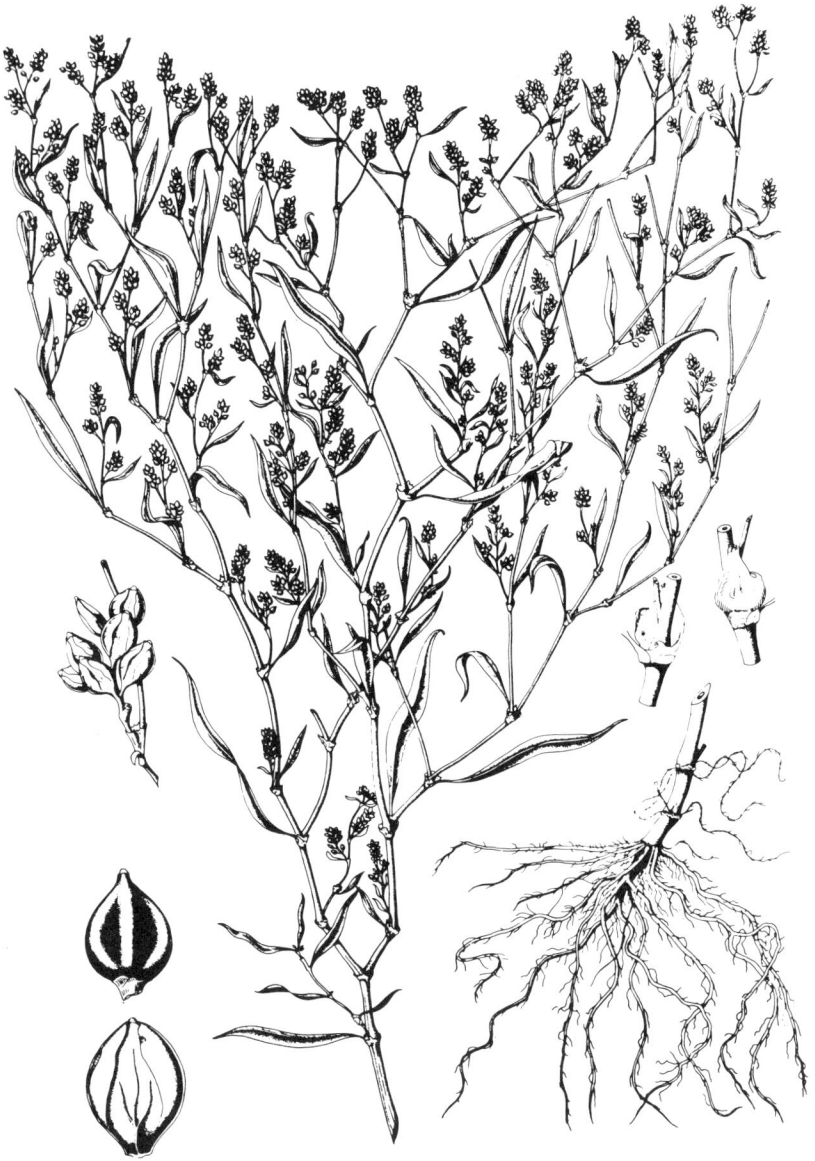

Lady's Thumb Smartweed

seeds are purplish-black and glossy. This European weed is very common in damp clearings.

Both of these smartweeds are annuals and there are no underground stems or creeping roots to contend with. Frequent mowing will prevent seed set, and thus eliminate plants. These weeds will not thrive where drainage is improved.

Prostrate knotweed (*Polygonum aviculare*), another annual herb in this family, is found frequently in lawns and known to cause dermatitis.

Young smartweeds are somewhat susceptible to foliar applications of certain herbicides, but older plants are resistant to herbicides.

Poisonous Plants
Water Hemlock

Cicuta maculata, also called poison hemlock and spotted cowbane, is a member of the parsley family and one of the most violently poisonous species in the United States. Its tuber-like, fleshy roots, which resemble small sweet potatoes and have the fragrance of parsnips, are deadly poisonous. While the roots and rootstocks are the most lethal portions, all parts of the plant contain some toxins (cicutoxin), especially when the plants are young.

Children and adults have eaten the fleshy roots, mistaking them for artichokes, parsnips, or other roots, with fatal results. Cattle, horses, and other domestic animals also have been poisoned by eating the roots. A piece of root the size of a walnut can kill a cow. The clusters of fleshy, fingerlike roots are shallowly embedded in soil, so the whole plant can easily be pulled out. When the roots are cut, a fragrant but poisonous yellow oil oozes from the cut surface. The stem is hollow between the joints, but the stem base has closely set partitions, as shown in the illustration. Children sometimes use the hollow stems to make whistles and are poisoned when they place the stems in their mouths.

The smooth stems, up to 6 or 7 feet tall, often are mottled with purple, especially in the lower parts. The leaves are alternate on the stem, and the veins of the leaf terminate in the notches at the margin. This characteristic differentiates water hemlock from another plant, *Angelica*, with which it often is confused. The veins of *Angelica* end in the teeth—not in the notches of the leaf—and the leaves generally are divided into three groups of three leaflets per leaf.

The white flowers are borne in an unbrella-like cluster and give rise to flattened fruits. Corky ridges alternating with oil tubes appear on the surfaces of the fruits.

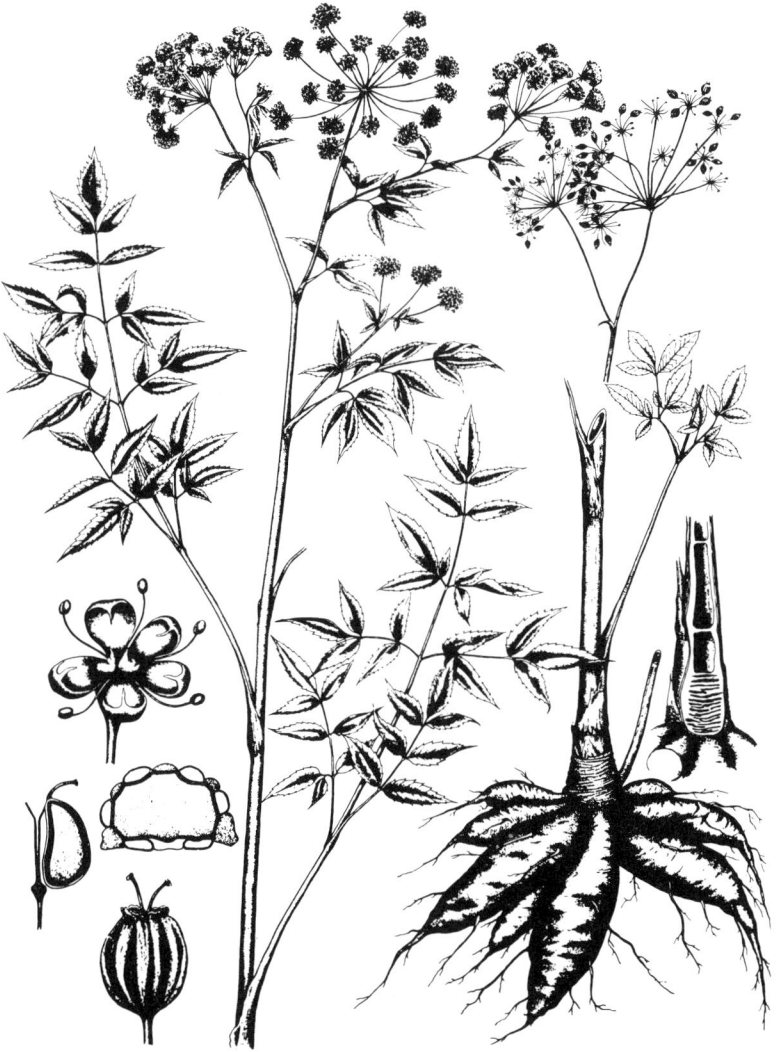

Water Hemlock

19

Symptoms of poisoning appear from 1 to several hours after eating the root, and include stomach pains, nausea, diarrhea, and dilation of the pupils. There are violent convulsions sometimes accompanied by frothing at the mouth. If emetics, followed by purgatives, are administered soon enough so that vomiting can be induced, the patient has a chance for recovery. Otherwise death can be sudden and is likely to occur during the convulsions. Death may occur in 15 minutes—or as long as 8 hours—after a lethal dose is taken. A physician should be called as soon as poisoning is suspected.

Water hemlock is easily destroyed by certain herbicides or by digging out the roots in this biennial plant. Marshes, ditches, wet streams, and lake borders near campsites and resort grounds should be checked carefully and all plants should be eradicated.

Water Parsnip

This perennial herb is native and widespread in North America and has been suspected of being poisonous to people and domestic animals. However, no toxic principle has been described. This plant can be readily distinguished from water hemlock because of the corrugated—or angled—stems and the different shape and grouping of leaflets, from 3 to 8 pairs per leaf, as illustrated.

Water parsnip (*Sium suave*) generally is branched above the middle and the leaves are alternate on the stems. The flowers and fruits are similar to those of water hemlock.

Plants grow in low swampy ground, meadows, muddy banks of streams, and even in standing water.

Other closely related plants are poison hemlock (*Conium maculatum*), which has white flowers and a fleshy, parsnip-like taproot, and wild parsnip (*Pastinaca sativa*). Poison hemlock causes a gradual paralysis of the lungs ending in death, but without convulsions. This was the poison used to end Socrate's life.

Wild parsnip, which has the fleshy tap root but yellow flowers, is not poisonous, although some persons get blistering of the skin from contact with the wet foliage, or become sensitive to sunlight. Wild carrot is not poisonous to people; however, if cows graze on it their milk can become tainted.

Water parsnip, like water hemlock and poison hemlock, can easily be pulled—or dug—from the soft earth in spring and destroyed. Or it can be killed with herbicides.

Water Parsnip

Jimsonweed

An ill-scented, dangerously poisonous weed, this plant is a stout, robust annual that produces both a nerve and stomach poison called hyoscyamine. Atropine and hyoscine are other alkaloids present. Jimsonweed (*Datura stramonium*) is in the same family as nightshade, potatoes, and petunias.

This bushy weed may grow 5 feet tall. Its stems are smooth and may be green or purple. The leaves are alternate, unevenly toothed, and strongly scented. The large, showy, trumpet-shaped flowers are white on the green-stemmed variety, and violet—or purplish—on the purple-stemmed variety. The fruit, borne in forks of branches, is a hard, prickly, four-parted capsule containing many large, flat, dark-brown or black seeds. At maturity the capsule bursts into four parts.

Domestic animals are poisoned by feeding on the tops of the plant. Children are poisoned by eating the unripe seed pods, which sometimes are called thorn apples. Some people are especially susceptible and get a skin rash from touching the leaves.

The nervous form of poisoning is most common. Its symptoms are headache, nausea, extreme thirst, a burning sensation of the skin, dilated pupils, hallucination, and loss of sight and control of limbs. In extreme cases, mania, convulsions, and death occur.

Jimsonweed grows in fields or waste places, mostly on rich, gravelly soils throughout the region. It should be mowed before seeds are produced. If mowed after fruits are ripe, the plants should be burned. Some herbicides will kill this rank weed.

Black Nightshade

Black or deadly nightshade (*Solanum nigrum* complex) belongs in the potato family and produces green berries in July and August. The unripe (green) berries are poisonous and contain the alkaloid solanine; the ripe berries (dull, purplish-black) may be nontoxic but not dependably so. The cultivated ''huckleberry'' or ''wonderberry'' is a close relative of this plant. Varieties exist that have nontoxic berries used in making jams. Leaves also contain solanine.

The plant, probably introduced from Europe or Asia, is an annual herb with somewhat angular stems. The leaves are alternate with wavy-toothed edges. The flowers are white and more or less clustered, with 5 to 10 flowers to a cluster.

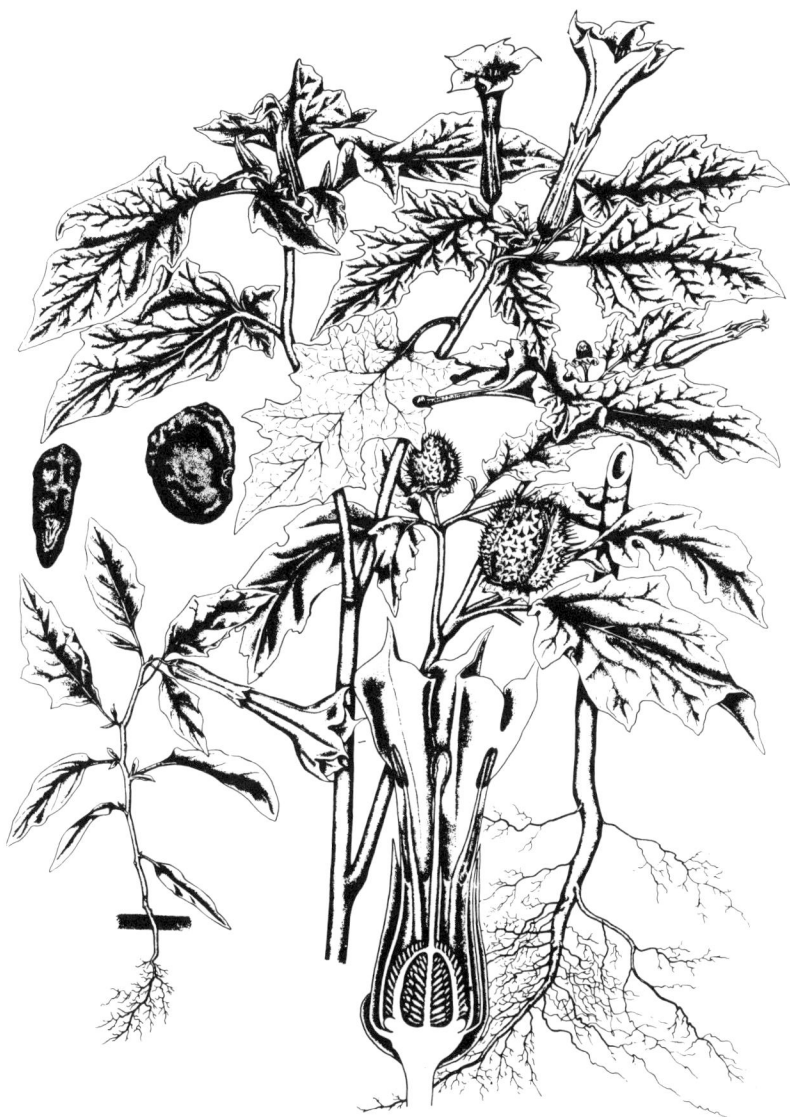

Jimsonweed

Black Nightshade

24

The Black Nightshade common to our region is Eastern Black Nightshade (*Solanum ptycanthum*). These plants inhabit waste places, fields, yards, campgrounds, or open woods—as well as croplands—and grow well on loam or gravelly soils.

Narcosis and paralysis occur from eating the unripe berries. This may show up first as a paralysis of the tongue and dilation of the pupils. If poisoning is suspected, an emetic should be given if a physician is not immediately available.

Plants can be easily eradicated by pulling them out by the roots or by hoeing. With young plants, repeated applications of certain herbicides provide control.

Poisonous Mushrooms

Of the more than 4,000 kinds of mushrooms known, at least several hundred kinds are large enough—and attractive enough in flavor and texture—to be gathered for eating. Most of these are edible; but some are toxic, causing symptoms ranging from discomfort to severe illness and death. Most cases of fatal mushroom poisoning result from consumption of species of *Amanita* (especially *A . verna* and *A . phalloides*), but several other species in other genera also contain toxins of different degrees or potency. A few kinds of mushrooms are mildly to strongly hallucinogenic. Unquestionably, edible kinds such as Inky Caps (*Coprinus*) and Morels (*Morchella*) when consumed with alcohol cause illness in some people. Many field and forest mushrooms, by the time they appear above the ground, are infested with the larvae of fungus flies. With the bacteria that accompany the larvae, the mushrooms may be unattractive or unwholesome. Edible mushrooms growing in lawns or fields, where pesticides have been applied, may not be suitable for food: they may take up enough of the chemicals to affect not only their flavor, but their edibility.

If wild mushrooms are to be gathered for eating, the sensible approach is to pick only fresh, sound specimens of those kinds known to be good and that can be identified with assurance.*

* *Mushrooms that can be eaten safely are listed in a guide called* Edible Wild Mushrooms. *To locate this guide and others, refer to the list of publications in the back of this book.*

25

Amanita Verna

Hayfever Plants

There are several causes of hayfever, but one major cause is plant pollen. In spring pollen comes primarily from trees. In summer it comes from grasses and plantains. In autumn it comes from ragweeds; primarily from the common ragweed (*Ambrosia artemisiifolia*) and the giant ragweed or kinghead (*Ambrosia trifida*). Both species are native annuals. They grow principally in moist waste places in the north central United States, except near the Great Lakes.

Common ragweed grows to 1 to 3 feet tall. It has mostly alternate leaves in the upper branches and opposite leaves in the lower parts of stems. The leaves are divided two or three times. Because there are no ray flowers, it may appear that the plant is not in flower and so does not produce pollen. But abundant pollen is produced on the petalless flowers. The nutlike fruits are up to $3/8$ inch long and have 4 to 7 short stout spines, plus a beak at one end.

Giant ragweed is a robust weed commonly 6 feet—and sometimes 15 feet—tall. The leaves are all opposite and three parted, except for the topmost leaves.

Mow in midsummer to prevent production of pollen and seed. Spray with herbicides to kill both ragweeds.

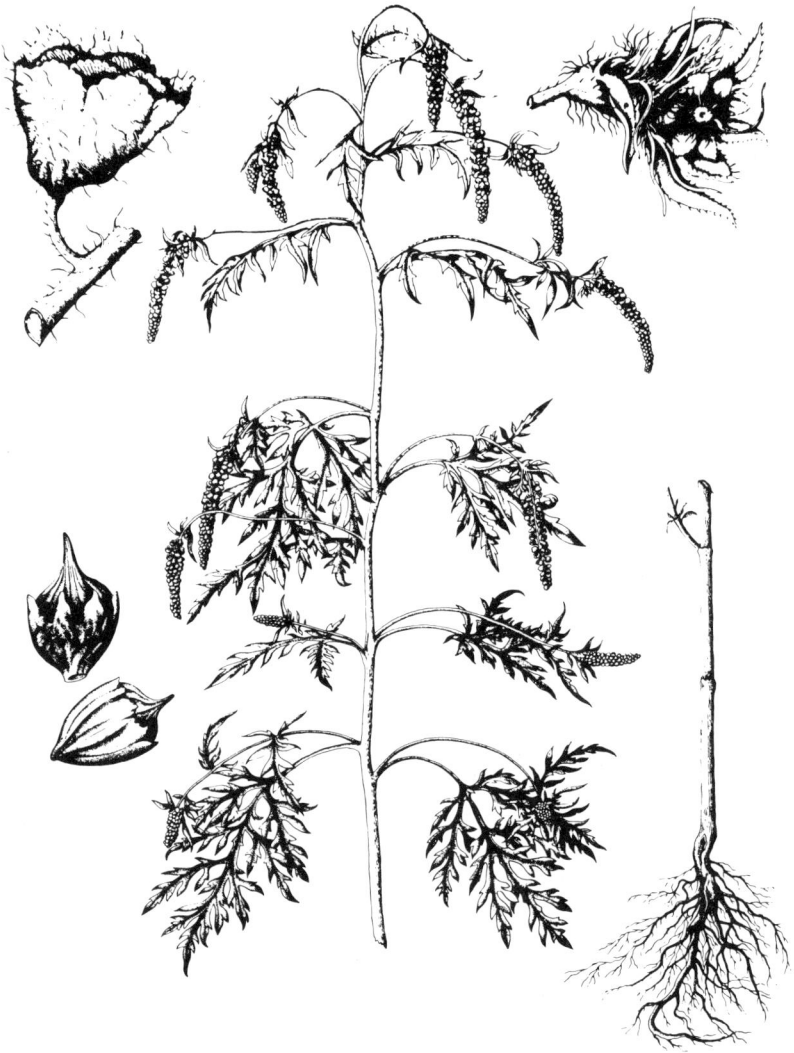

Common Ragweed

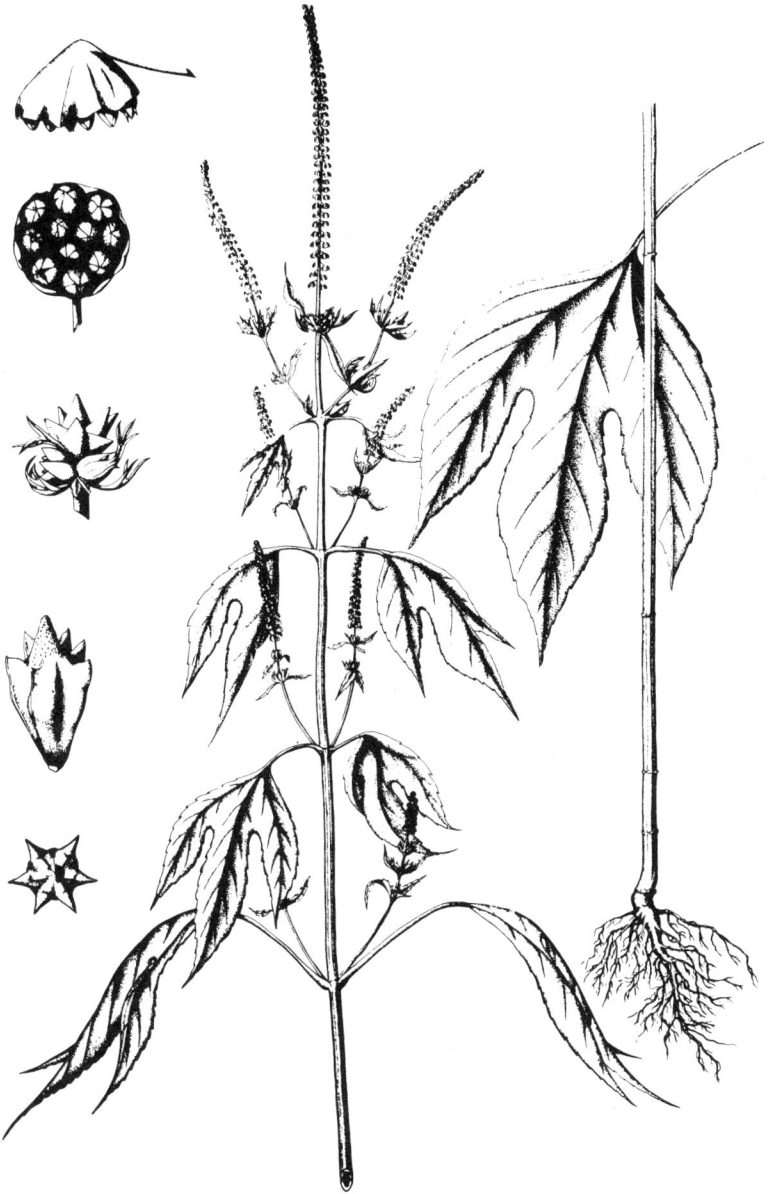

Giant Ragweed

Plants with Thorny Fruits
Sandbur

The sandbur (*Cenchrus longispinus*) produces a bur with spines stout enough to penetrate the flesh of humans and animals.

This much-branched, annual grass weed often spreads by taking root at the lower joints of the stem. The sheaths that enclose the stems are loose and often overlap. The usually flat leaves are about 1/4 inch wide, and there is a fringe of hairs where the leaf blade joins the sheath around the stem. The grass flower is enclosed by a hairy, spiny bur composed of many bristles, each provided with recurved barbs. It is these barbs that enable the spines to work into the flesh. Seeds in the bur can live in soil for 4 years and probably live longer.

Because it is an annual plant, reproduction occurs only from seeds contained in the burs. Moreover, infestation can occur from burs carried on people, or animals, or from burs floating along the shore from place to place.

These spines can result in inflammation and infection of the punctured skin. The burs mix with sand on the beach, ready to puncture the skin of swimmers or sunbathers. Often the spines break off when the bur is jerked from the flesh, so tweezers must be used to extract the severed spine of the bur. The burs also adhere to clothing or get entangled in the fur of domestic animals.

Eradication is possible by burning the burs with a flame burner with the flame directed at the tops of the plants. Because burs are pro-

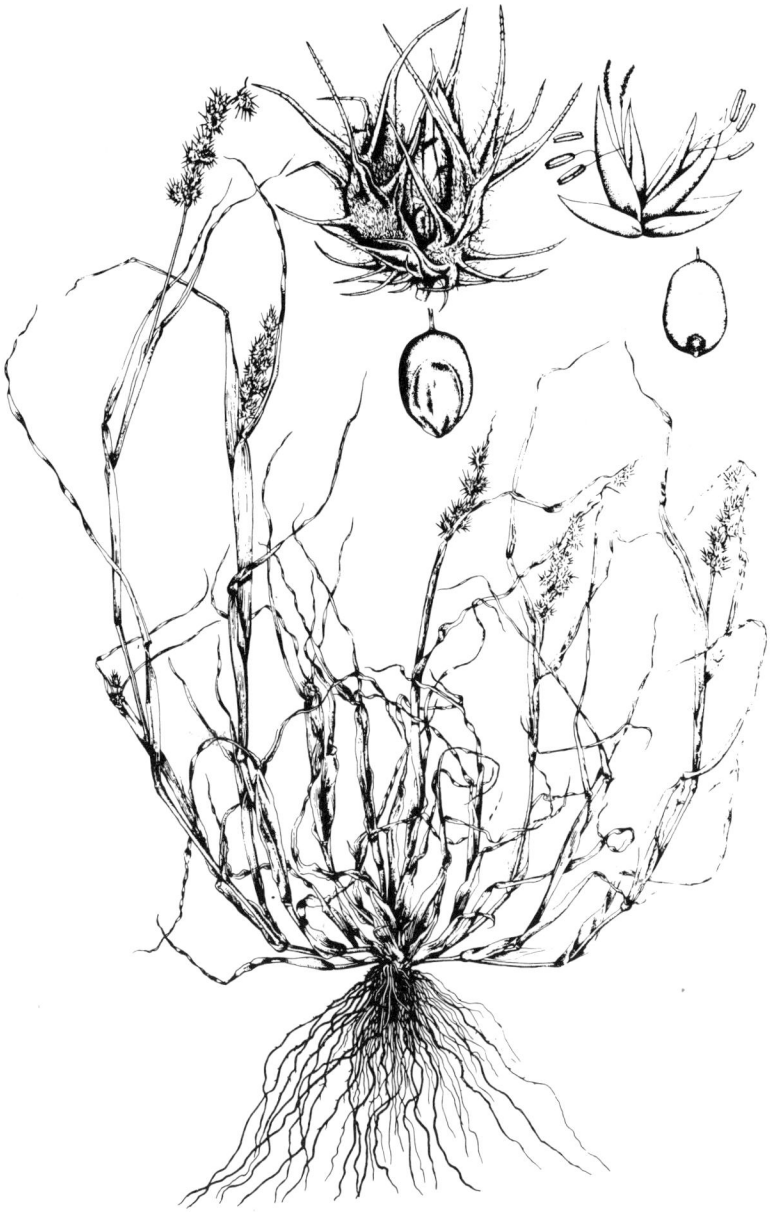

Sandbur

duced so close to the ground, mowing is ineffective in eradicating sandbur.

For chemical control on beaches or pathways, any of the accepted grass killing herbicides can be used. Some chemicals will kill sandbur, but can cause skin irritation if bathers lie in the sand shortly after the chemicals have been applied. Remember that these herbicides will kill many other grasses also, so they should not be used to kill sandbur when it is with desirable grasses. In that case, the best control is to make sure you have good black soil and maintain a healthy, vigorous lawn.

Beggarticks

Hunters, hikers, and late summer or autumn campers are united in their dislike of this robust weed. Two downwardly barbed spines at one end of each seed of beggarticks (*Bidens frondosa*) cling tenaciously to clothing and are difficult to remove, especially from woolens. Moreover, it has only minor value as food for wildlife.

Spanish needle, devil's pitchfork, sticktight, and bur marigold are other names for this weed. Plants on lakeshores may vary—from a few inches to 5 feet or more—in height. The plant is an annual with opposite leaves that are divided into many leaflets. The leaf margin is fine toothed.

The yellow to orange-yellow flowers are conspicuous in late summer. Below the head of flowers there are 2 rows—or series—of very small leaves. The blackish seeds are borne on a flat, chaffy disc and are more or less four-sided.

Beggarticks grow in damp, open areas, along lakeshores, and sometimes even in relatively dry waste places. Improving the drainage on moist land helps to control this weed. Mowing before seed formation will prevent infestation of the land. Spraying with a number of herbicides also will control this plant.

Stickseed

This grayish, hairy, bluish-flowered plant produces many small fruits that are covered with prickles. Common stickseed (*Lappula echinata*) grows 1 to 2 feet high on dry locations in full sunlight. Virginia stickseed (*Hackelia virginiana*) is found in moist and shaded sites where it is usually 2 to 4 feet high. Common stickweed has hairy leaves 3/4 to 3 inches long and 1/8 to 1/4 inch wide. The flowers are blue, and the plant sometimes is called blue bur. Virginia stickseed has

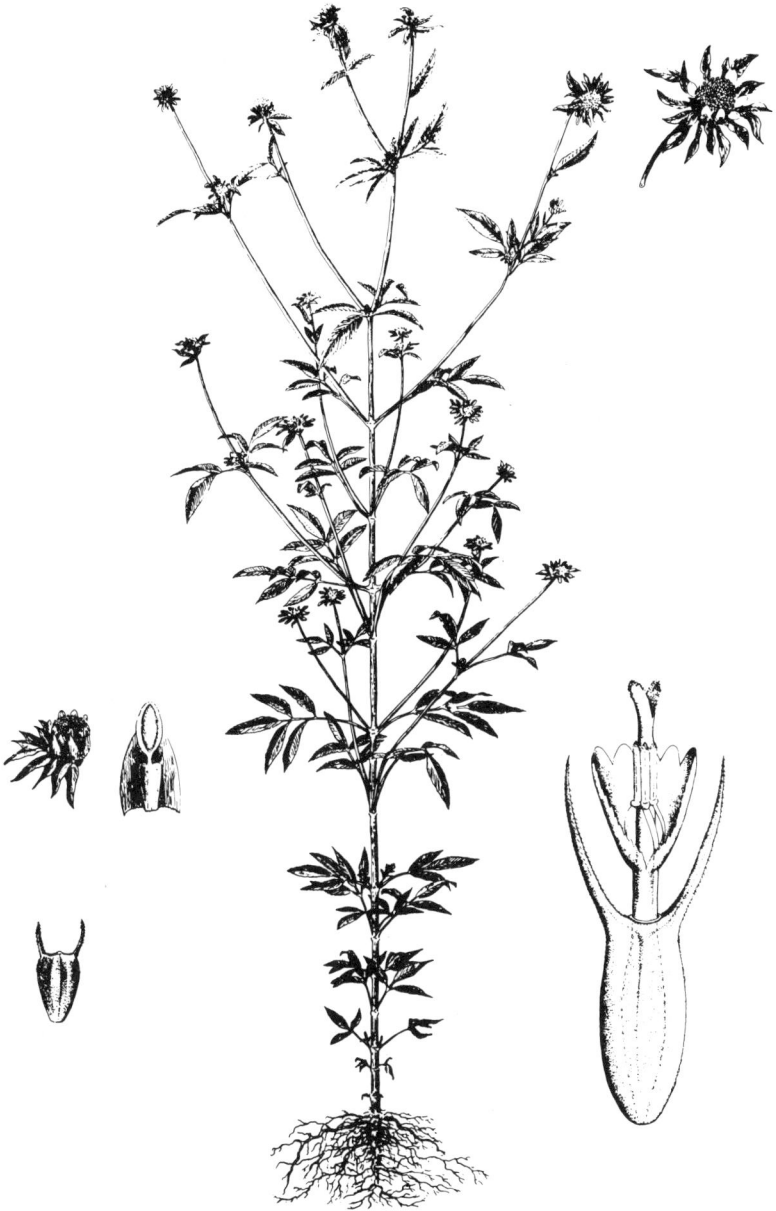

Beggar's Ticks

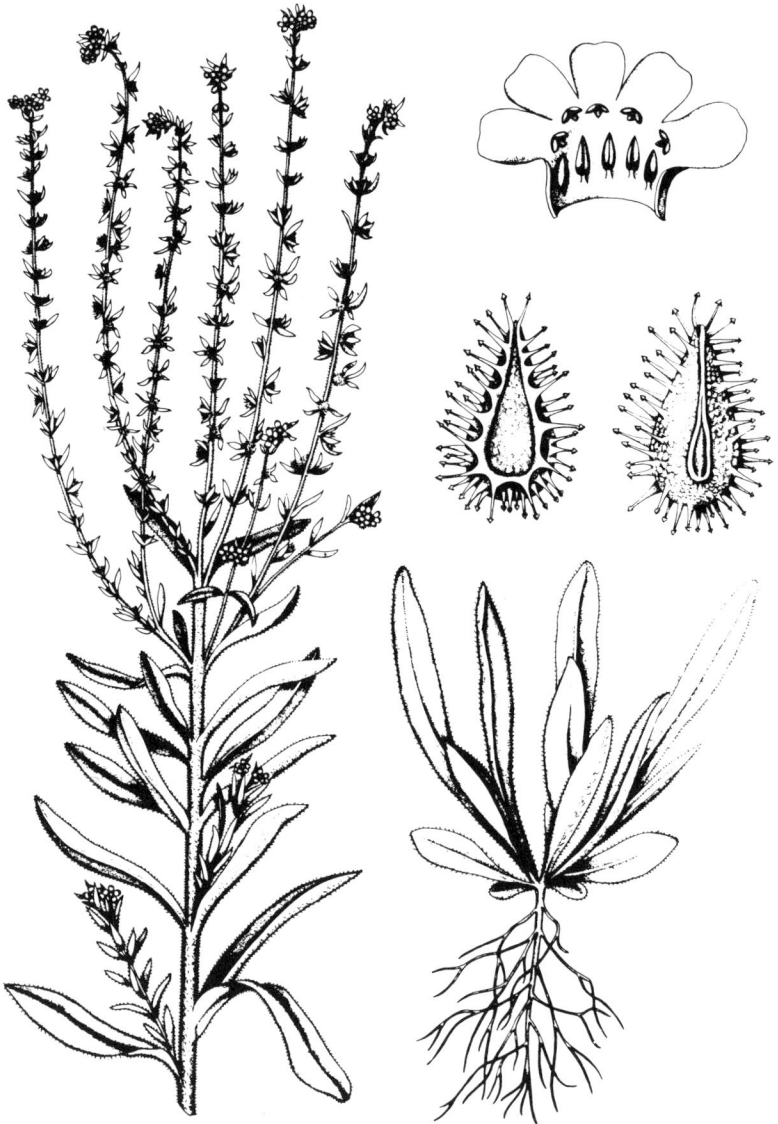

Stickseed

Virginia Stickseed

35

larger, smooth leaves and flowers that vary from pale blue to white. The stems of both species are erect, simple, slender, and branched at the top. Leaves are alternate, undivided, oblong to narrow, have smooth margins, and are without stalks.

The fruit of these species is a cluster of four small, erect nutlets about ⅛ inch long with a double row of barbed prickles around the margin. These prickly nutlets stick in the wool and hair of animals, and to clothing. The name sticktight sometimes is used for the plant. These species are annuals or winter annuals that reproduce by seed.

Both stickseeds generally grow in waste places that are not mowed or cultivated regularly. They may be controlled by cutting the rosette stage below the ground (with a hoe) in fall or early spring. Mowing the plants before they produce seed will prevent formation of the prickly burs and reduce the seed for future generations. Certain herbicides usually provide effective control.

Tick Trefoil

This plant, sometimes also called beggarticks, but more commonly called tick trefoil or tick clover is one of several species of *Desmodium*. One example is *Desmodium canadense*. These plants are perennials of the legume family; having three-part leaves like clover, and often having rose-colored, pea-like flowers.

The plant produces a flat, deeply-jointed pod that separates into 3 to 6 joints, each containing one seed. The surface of the pod is covered with hooked hairs. The seeds are about ⅛ inch long, kidney shaped, and a dull, reddish-brown.

There are many wild species of *Desmodium* that grow in woodlands and spread on to neighboring open lands or pastures.

Mowing will prevent seed production, but will not eradicate the plant unless repeated often. Tick trefoils are not easily killed by chemicals.

Cocklebur

Many a pheasant hunter has cursed this coarse annual weed because of the rough burs that hook or tear clothing, or cling to the fur of animals. The farmer also has reason to eradicate cocklebur (*Xanthium strumarium*), since the burs get tangled in the wool of sheep—or injure the hide of farm animals—making infection possible. Also, the first seed leaves that emerge in the spring have been reported to be poisonous to some farm animals.

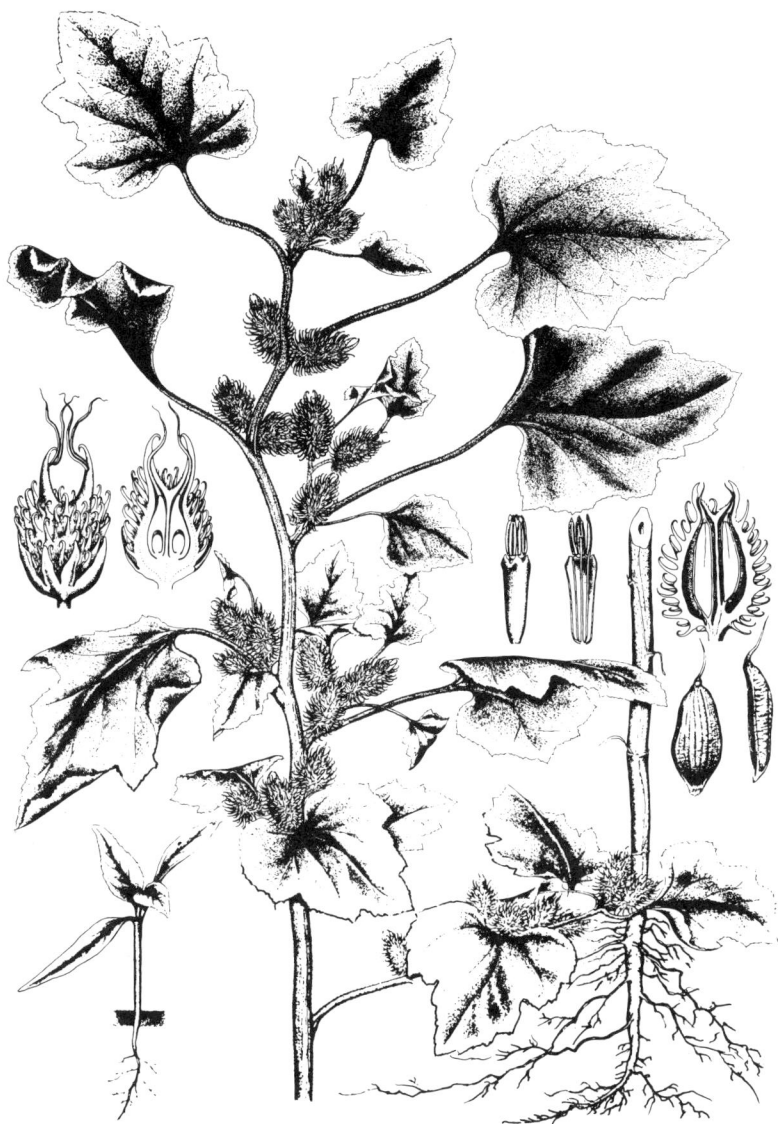

Cocklebur

The stem of cocklebur is somewhat rough, angled, and frequently spotted with red. The large, alternate leaves vary from heart-shaped to nearly kidney-shaped.

Because of the variation in the shape, hairiness, and spininess of mature burs, many forms or species have been described. In general, the burs have 2 stout, incurved hooks at one end. Often the hooks on ripe fruits are reddish-tinged. Each bur is 2 chambered with a flattish seed in each chamber. For the species described here, there are about 100 to150 prickles on one face of the bur.

Cocklebur frequently grows on lowlands, lake beaches, or on wastelands.

Plants should be mowed to prevent seed formation, or they can be killed by spraying them with herbicides.

Burdock

The large, bristly burs of this biennial (*Arctium minus*) are a major nuisance to those who walk in uncultivated fields, or tend domestic animals that have ventured too close to patches of it. The fur—or hair—of animals becomes thoroughly matted with the prickly fruits of this relative of garden rhubarb.

In the first year of growth, a rosette of leaves resembling rhubarb (in size and growth habit) is produced. Fruiting occurs in the second year, when numerous many-seeded burs await the chance encounter with people—or animals—to be dispersed. The spines have hooked ends that enable them to be carried about by animals.

The large, fleshy taproot produced the first year contains stored food for the fruiting year. The rough, hairy leaves of the rosette often measure a foot in length. The pinkish-purple flowers arise from shoots growing just above the place on the stem where leaves are attached. Neglected farmyards, fence rows, or rich soils of uncultivated areas of campgrounds or fields are favorite habitats for this weed. Plants can be eradicated by cultivation, especially during the first year. Spraying with certain herbicides also will control burdock.

Burdock

Plants with Thorny Stems

Prickly Ash

One of two species of the citrus family native to this region is prickly ash (*Xanthoxylum americanum*). It is a large shrub or small tree, measuring up to 12 feet in height, with thorny stems that easily deter even the experienced hunter or hiker from attempting to go through a thicket of them.

This shrub reproduces by seeds, and by the production of horizontal roots. Stems, branches, and twigs have thorns up to 1/2 inch long. The thorns occur in pairs at the bases of leaves.

The compound leaves bear from 2 to 4 pairs of leaflets, plus an odd one. Young leaves are downy. As they mature they become nearly smooth on the upper surface but remain hairy on the lower surface. The leaves are rather thick and dotted with translucent oil glands. While the leaves and fruits are pleasantly aromatic, the taste is disagreeably pungent. The flowers are yellowish green, and open before the leaves appear.

The fruit is somewhat fleshy and becomes reddish- brown when mature. The black, shiny seeds are about 1/8 inch long.

40

Prickly Ash

41

Prickly ash inhabits thickets, riverbanks, and thick, moist woods and frequently thrives at edges of woodlands.

Control of these thorny shrubs can be accomplished by grubbing out the roots, or by application of brush killers. Repeated applications may be necessary.

Prickly Greenbrier

Hunters, and others who tramp through unpastured woodlands, may find themselves entangled in the thorny and unyielding vine of greenbrier (*Smilax hispida*). The spines are black, very firm, and usually ¼ to ½ inch long. They may tear clothing, or inflict wounds on unprotected skin. Even in winter the stem is a bright green, which makes the plant readily identifiable.

The plants are not common. They occur in woodlands as scattered clumps that climb on other plants, thriving on rich, moist soil in most of our north central states. They attain a length of up to 20 feet. Several stems arise from a common rootstock. A pair of tendrils occurs at the base of each leaf.

The leaves are thin, vary from oval to heart shaped, and usually have 5 to 7 prominent veins per leaf.

Six to twenty flowers are clustered at the bases of leaves. The berries are bluish-black.

Greenbrier can be controlled by grubbing out the rootstocks or by application of certain herbicides at the bases of plants.

Buffalo Bur

This noxious annual weed of the potato family has poisonous, prickly berries and prickly stems. The stiff yellow spines on its stems and fruit are so sharp that even animals will not touch the plant. The spines are easily detachable and become imbedded in human skin if one brushes against them. The plant is native to our western states but has been introduced into the midwest in feed, screenings, and hay. Buffalo bur (*Solanum rostratum*) frequently occurs first in the vicinity of feedlots. From there it spreads to cultivated fields and to uncultivated areas.

Stems of the buffalo bur are erect but have many branches and are somewhat spreading. When mature, the plant often breaks at the ground line and is blown around like a tumble weed. It is generally about 1 foot tall, but may reach 2 feet. Leaves are alternate on the stem and are deeply lobed, similar to watermelon leaves. The leaf surface is

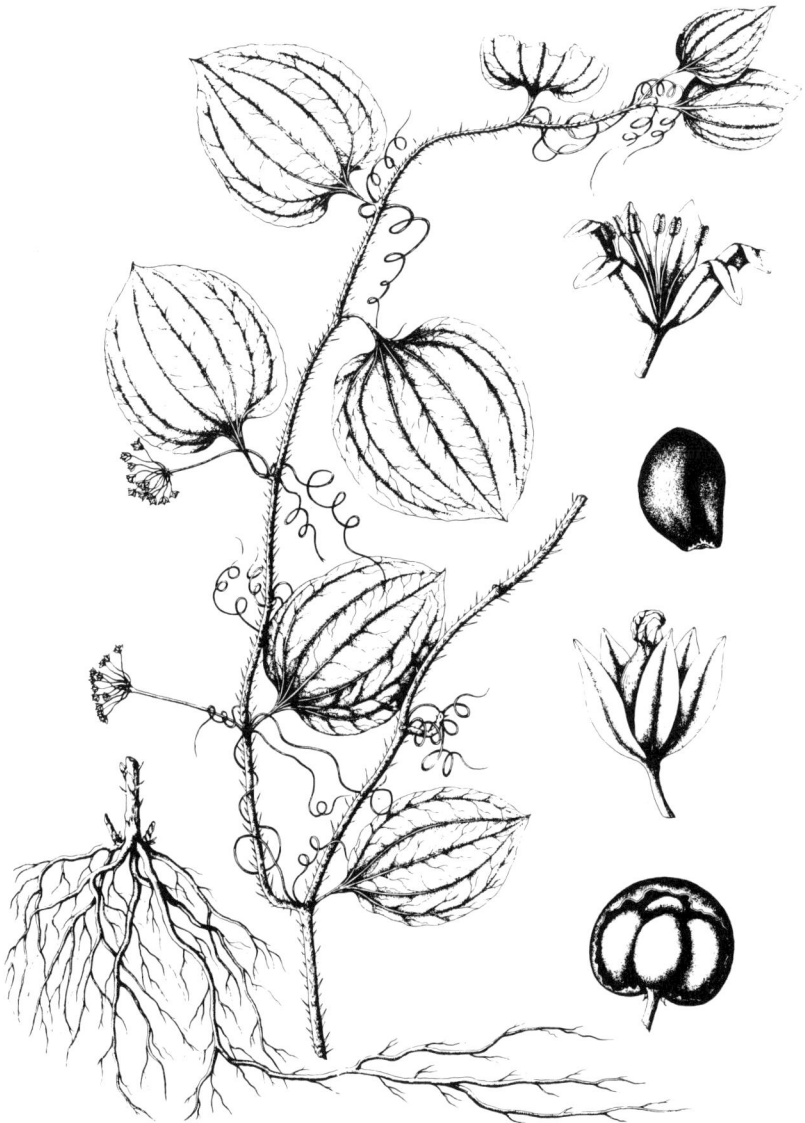

Prickly Greenbrier

43

Buffalo Bur

covered with hair; veins, midribs, and leaf stems are prickly. The yellow, wheel-shaped flowers—about 1 inch in diameter and similar to those of tomato—are borne in clusters on prickly stems. The fruit is a berry encased in a spiny covering.

These plants can be controlled by clean cultivation, or by mowing waste areas in which they grow, to prevent them from producing seed. Selective weed control chemicals generally are not effective.

Horse Nettle

This close relative of buffalo bur is not only a pest as a weed in spring, but also has poisonous leaves and berries. In addition, it is susceptible to tomato mosaic, which makes it objectionable near tomato fields. Horse nettle (*Solanum carolinense*) is not poisonous in all growth stages but—because the presence or absence of the poison cannot be known at all times—it should never be eaten.

This perennial weed spreads by creeping rootstocks that are up to 3 feet long. Vertical taproots penetrate to depths of 8 feet. It is troublesome in meadows or in crops, especially on loose, sandy soils.

The stems, petioles, fruiting stalks, and leaf midribs-and-veins are thinly covered with stout, yellowish spines, as in buffalo bur. The stout, erect stems are loosely branched and reach a height of 8 to 24 inches. Short stiff hairs fill in the space between the spines on the stems. Leaves are shaped like those of white oak, having shallow cuts and rounded lobes covered with hairs. Flowers are pale violet to white on a flower stalk. The fruit is an orange-colored, smooth berry that contains 40 to 60 seeds.

This plant can be controlled in fields by clean cultivation. It can be choked out on campgrounds or in resort areas by establishing a good sod of bluegrass. Horse nettle patches should be mowed in uncultivated areas to prevent seed formation.

The application of herbicides is not always effective; however, a few have given some favorable results.

Canada Thistle

This deep-rooted perennial thistle has been declared noxious in the seed laws of at least 43 states. Canada thistle (*Cirsium arvense*) thrives in almost every state in the north central area, especially the northern-most states. Its prickly leaves and stems are a nuisance in camp and resort areas.

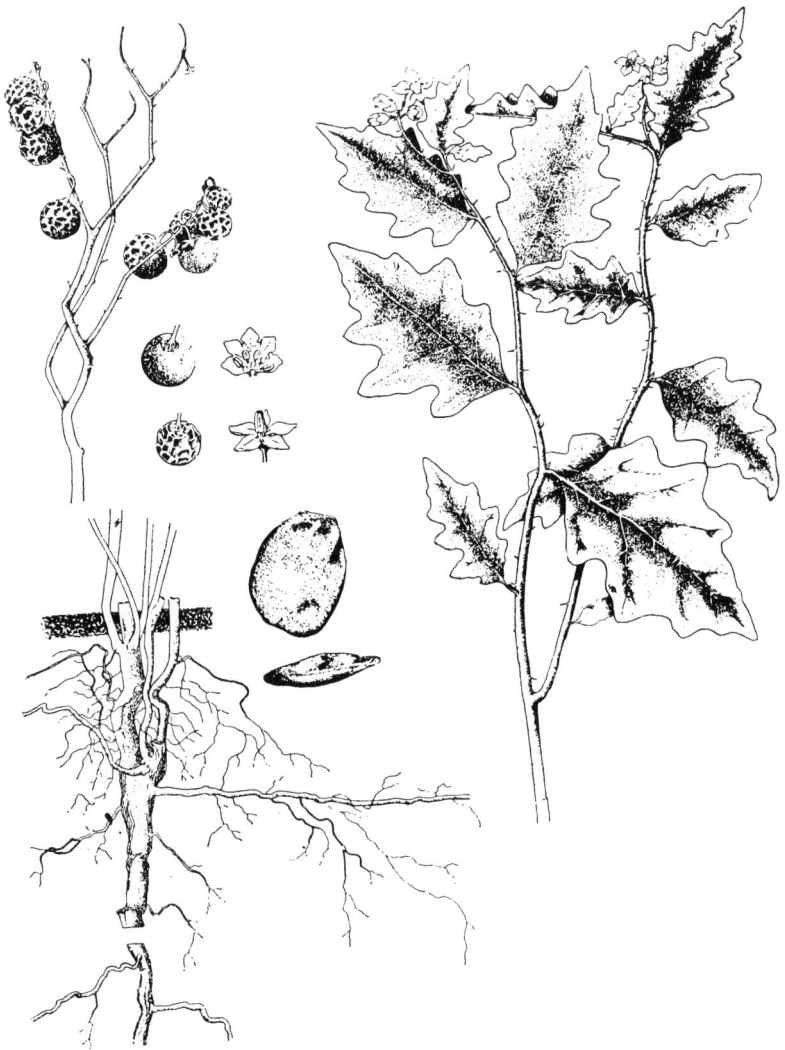

Horse Nettle

Canada Thistle

While the major portion of the (extensively creeping and freely sprouting) roots lies within a foot of the soil surface, roots can penetrate to depths of 6 to 8 feet or more, especially in loose, well drained soil. New shoots can arise from creeping roots from a depth of 8 inches. For example, in 3 years' time, a three-inch cutting of Canada thistle can produce a patch 60 feet in diameter. Every piece of the creeping root system can give rise to a new plant.

The stems are ridged and very leafy. The lower surfaces of leaves are either smooth or somewhat woolly. The leaves—which are alternate—are irregularly lobed and spiny on the margins; although one variety is not lobed and is almost without prickles.

Flower color varies from white to pink, lavender, and rose-purple. The flowers on a given plant are all male —or all female—but occasionally both sexes can be found in one flower. Of course, there is no seed from male plants—or from female plants—located far away from male plants.

Lack of seed also is caused by the attack of certain insects, notably the Canada thistle midge, or the larvae of fruit flies. Often the whole flower head may turn brown from insect attacks.

While Canada thistle grows nearly everywhere, it is especially abundant on rich or heavy soils.

The food reserves in the roots are lowest about the first week in June, so mowing the plants at this time forces the plant to use up what little food still is available for the production of new shoots. Plants cut while in flower often will continue to ripen, but the seed is not viable.

Usually several applications of certain herbicides, each year for several years, are necessary for control of Canada thistle. For small patches, soil sterilants can be used successfully.

Bull Thistle

An aggressive, fiercely-armed weed of clearings, bull thistle (*Cirsium vulgare*)—also named common and spear thistle—is a biennial plant that produces a prickly rosette of leaves the first year, and a spiny-winged, flowering stem the second year.

This alien weed produces a fleshy taproot, which later becomes spindle shaped. The plant overwinters with no stem appearing above the ground, only a rosette of leaves that are pale, woolly, or webbed beneath and green-and-smooth above. The lobes bear long, stout prickles.

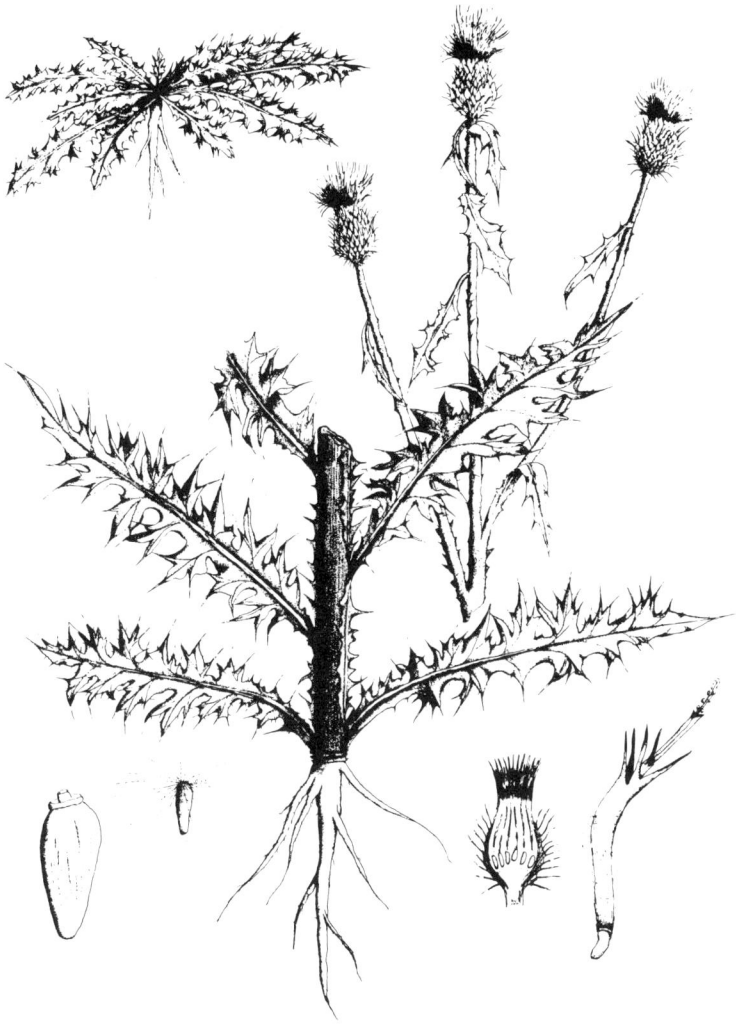

Bull Thistle

49

In the second year a woolly, furrowed, prickly-lobed, and very leafy stem appears. The leaves are alternate, and are woolly and spiny like the rosette leaves.

Unlike those in Canada thistle, the heads are solitary, or there are only a few at the tips of short, prickly, winged branches. The purple flowers produce seeds 1/8 inch or longer. They are straw colored with grayish-black stripes.

Bull thistle will not persist under cultivation or mowing, and also can be killed by repeated applications of herbicides.

Roadside Thistle

This spiny thistle closely resembles bull thistle; except it is less prickly and usually branches only near the summit, and not at the base of the stem. It is not as tall and robust as the tall thistle (*Cirsium altissimum*), which it resembles even more closely.

Although sometimes a perennial, roadside thistle (*Cirsium discolor*) usually is a biennial. The first year's rosette leaves are stalked, green-and-smooth above, but white-felted beneath; whereas, bull thistle is more coarsely woolly. Also, the leaf of roadside thistle is divided nearly to the midrib making bristly-toothed lobes.

The heads, mostly solitary, are borne on leafy branches of the strongly ribbed flowering stem. While flowers usually are purple, some white-flowered forms occasionally appear.

Cultivation and mowing, or repeated applications of herbicides, will control roadside thistle.

Trailing Bramble

This prickly, trailing bramble (*Rubus flagellaris*), known also as dewberry, and running or wild blackberry, is a woody perennial that frequents openings and borders of thickets. It is responsible for scratching the arms or legs of many campers or hunters. Many an outdoor person has been tripped by the trailing canes of this and other brambles.

The stems, or canes, produced the first year are long, creeping, and prostrate, and usually root at the tips. Prickles on these canes measure more than 1/8 inch in length. In the second year an erect—or sometimes trailing— flowering cane that is woody, tough, and often reddish, or purplish, is produced. The leaves of first year canes consist of 3 to 5 leaflets; the second year canes produce leaves of 3 leaflets. Veins may be hairy on the under surface of the leaf, at least on first year canes. The white blossoms appear in late May or June. The fruit ripens in August, is about $1/2$ inch in diameter, and has a rich flavor that makes it suitable for use in jam.

This highly variable species occurs widely in the north central region, chiefly on acid soils, sands or gravels; and in dry fields, clearings, and edges of thickets. It is difficult to identify species in this group.

Because the canes are so long and tangled it is difficult to eradicate these plants by grubbing. Most other bramble or blackberry species are not so thorny, and can be more easily grubbed out.

Brush killers have been reported to be successful eradicators.

Other Prickly Plants

Cuts, scratches, and torn stockings rank high among the irritations that sometimes accompany the delights of Sunday afternoon strolling, picnicking, or hiking. Among such wound-inflicting plants are cleavers (*Galium aparine*), also called bedstraw, and arrow-leaf thumb (*Polygonum sagittatum*). These plants, although unrelated botanically, are similar in having weak, four-angled stems that often lean on other kinds of plants nearby. Cleavers grow frequently in openings of rich woods or thickets, whereas tearthumb is found on low ground. Both are annuals and reproduce by seeds.

Cleavers have a wiry, ridged stem with short, bristly hooks along the ridges. The narrow, bristle-tipped leaves are generally grouped 6 to 8 at a stem joint, and are tapered toward the base. Even the fruit is bristly and is produced from white-petalled flowers.

Tearthumb is characterized by having stiff barbs on the branches, on mid-veins of leaves, and along the upper parts of stems. The arrow-shaped leaves are not grouped as in cleavers, but occur singley and are arranged alternately on the stem. The flowers may be white or pink and the fruits are three-angled.

52

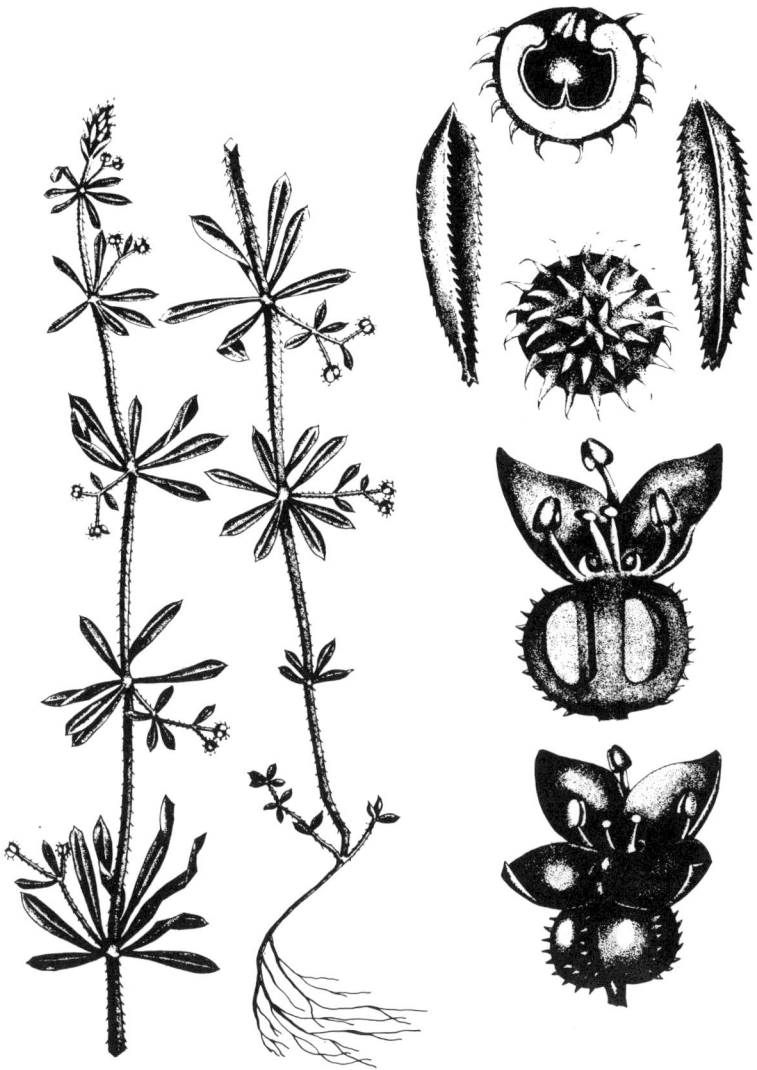

Cleavers

53

Arrow-leaf Tearthumb

54

These plants should be raked out before seed sets; cleavers especially are so loosely attached to the soil that just walking through a patch of them is enough to dislodge them from the soil or humus and whole plants may adhere to clothing.

In swamps, ditches, and along the shores of lakes or streams, one may encounter rice cut-grass (*Leersia oryzoides*) with memorable results. The leaves, not stems, have saw-toothed edges that can gash unprotected skin. Often the veins on the underside of leaves also are harsh and rough. This grass reproduces by seeds and by rootstocks.

Grass-killing herbicides can be applied to rice cut-grass but other grass species in the vicinity will also be affected.

Rice Cut-grass

Water Plants

Aquatic plants often are considered weeds because they obstruct boating, or swimming, or make fishing difficult. However, since weedy lakes produce more food for fish than bare-open regions, some water plants are necessary for fish to live and grow. But there may be waters that are so weedy even fish do not develop properly. Because fish are involved, any chemical-control method for water weeds usually must have the approval of the state department of conservation or natural resources. A permit is issued by the appropriate state department.

Usually, only licensed commercial operators are permitted to treat submerged vegetation since the chemical used is dangerous to people—and fish—and is expensive to use. However, there are mechanical methods of controlling aquatic vegetation. Address inquiries concerning the control of aquatic plants to the local state departments involved.

Hornwort (Coontail)

Hornwort (*Ceratophyllum demersum*) is one of the most common and widely distributed submerged aquatic plants.

Viewed through the water, the plant appears to be olive green. No roots are produced, even by seedlings. In its early growth stages the lower end often is anchored in mud, giving the appearance of being rooted. Later, the stems float on—or near—the surface of the water.

56

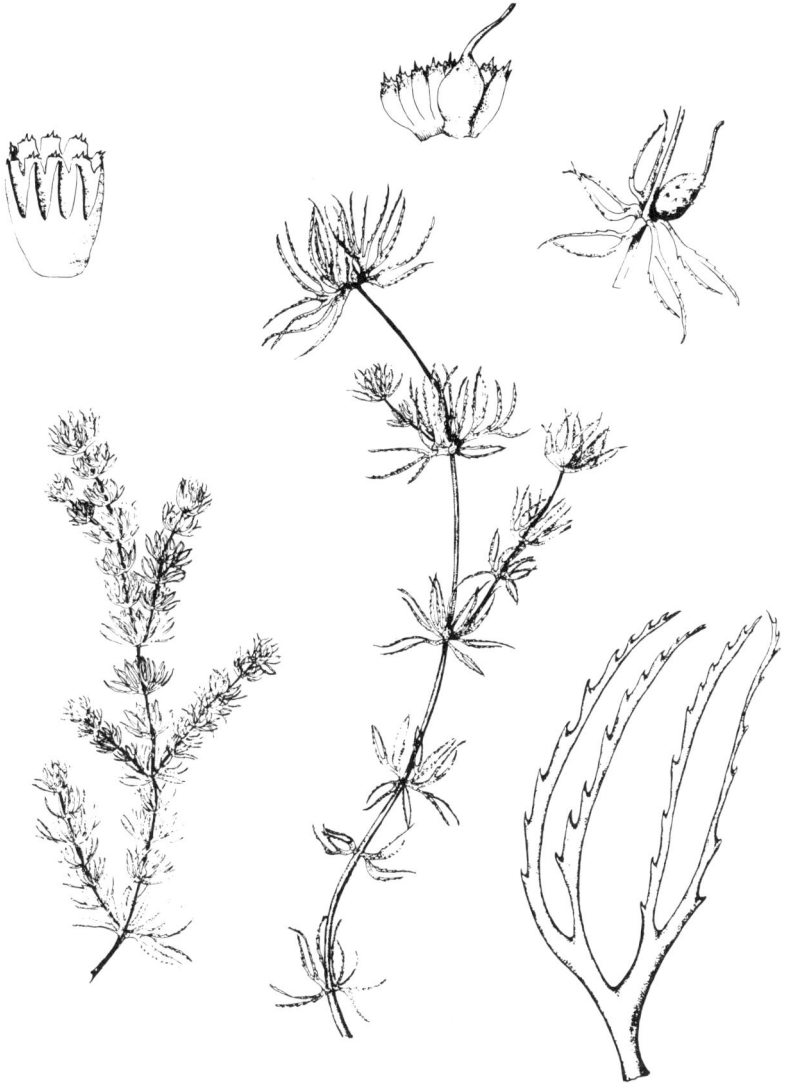

Hornwort (Coontail)

57

The coarse stems are brittle and stiffly branching, or they may be ropelike and flexuous. The leaves are in whorls, with 5 to 12 leaves in a group; each of which is again divided into 2 or 3 thread-like segments with teeth along one side of each segment. The leaves often are more densely crowded toward the ends of the branches. For this reason, the plant often is called coontail.

It is especially irritating to swimmers because of the rough, scratchy surface of its leaves and stems. It also is one of the most objectionable water plants growing offshore along beaches.

Flowers are rarely seen and seeds are produced in late summer or early fall. Although eaten by ducks, the seed is not regarded as a choice food. But the plants do provide shelter for young fish.

Hornwort is found in quiet lakes, shallow ponds, and slow streams—especially if bottoms are muddy. It apparently is most abundant in hard water.

Water Milfoil

The cut-leaf, coarse, submerged water plant (*Myriophyllum verticillatum*) can be mistaken for hornwort. The major difference is in the leaf margins of the submerged leaves.

There is an abrupt transition from submerged to emerged leaves, as the leaf division is much coarser in emerged leaves. The submerged leaves are more than 1 inch long and are divided into 9 to 13 segments. Unlike hornwort, the segments of the milfoil leaves are not toothed.

The robust stems arise from creeping rootstalks and emerge as much as 5 inches above the water surface. They root freely at the lower joints.

Many species of milfoil are almost exactly alike except for flowers and fruit, which makes it difficult to identify species.

This aquatic weed is, at best, a low grade food for ducks. It grows in the shallow, quiet water of limestone—or clay—areas, and in the shallow bays of lakes, near the edges of currents entering the lakes from streams.

Waterweed

Waterweed (*Elodea canadensis*), a submerged, perennial weed of waterways, can clog bays, ponds, and lagoons. The sticky, slimy leaves are annoying to swimmers. The brittle stems break easily and add to the debris washed ashore.

Water Milfoil

59

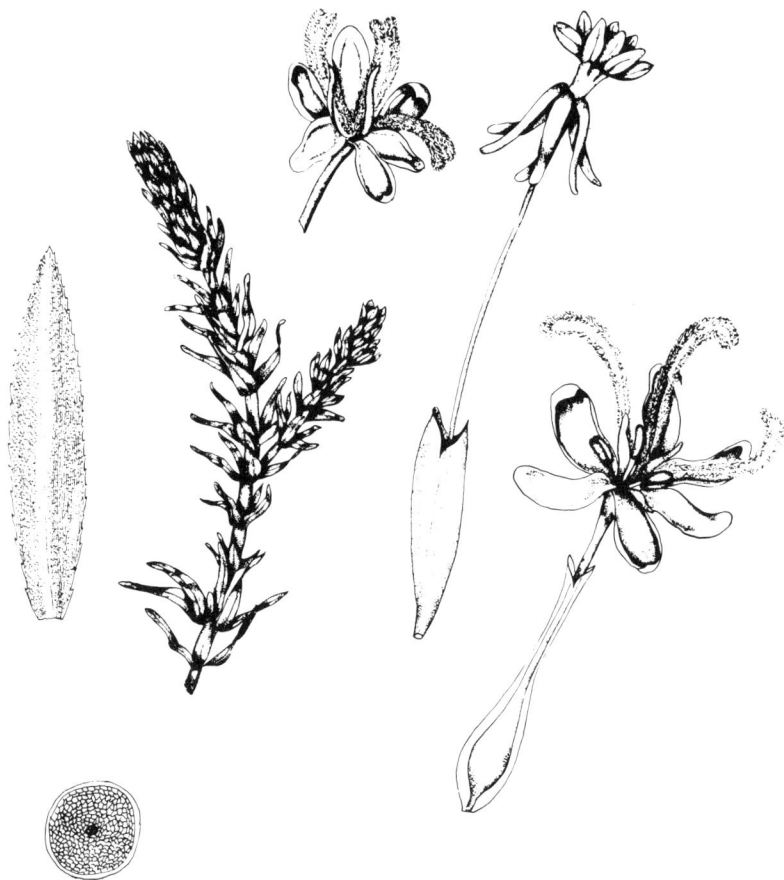

Waterweed

The roots are fibrous and the plants, which are 1 to 3 feet long, often are rooted at the bottom of the lake. Stem fragments sometimes can be found floating in mats on the surface. The leaves frequently are tinged with purple.

These plants are common in the hard waters of lakes, ponds, and slow-moving streams.

Pondweeds

The dominant vegetation in thousands of our lakes is pondweed (*Potamogeton* spp.). There are so many species in this family—the largest of the aquatic seed plants—that they will be described as a group.

Pondweeds in general are jointed herbs with mostly rooting stems and two-ranked leaves. They grow from lake beds at depths of 4 to 12 feet, sending out long floating branches on, or near, the water surface. The submerged leaves are grass-like and transparent, while the floating leaves are shorter, broader, oval, and generally of a more leathery texture.

In sheltered bays, pondweeds may grow in dense patches. Wave action may wash fragments of pondweeds to shore.

A few common pondweeds are illustrated: sago pondweed (*Potamogeton pectinatus*), which bears tubers on rootstocks and has bristle-shaped leaves; floating pondweed (*Potamogeton natans*), which has red-spotted rootstocks, ridged stems, and floating leaves; and clasping leaved pondweed (*Potamogeton perfoliatus*), in which the leaves are clasping and the veins are prominent.

Bulrushes

Bulrushes (*Scirpus* spp.) are widely distributed in ponds, lakes, wet swales, and marshes. Floating vegetation may lodge in the rushes, producing objectionable odors when decaying. But the odor probably is due to bacteria or blue-green algae.

The bulrushes are annuals or perennials and vary in height from a few inches to several feet. If perennial, thick stands are produced from root-stocks.

River bulrush (*Scirpus fluviatilis*) is common in sloughs, along the borders of ponds, and in the bays of large lakes. The great bulrush (*Scirpus validus*) grows in shallow ponds, especially around spring holes, bog holes, and stream banks. Other rushes also are common in the region.

Sago Pondweed

Floating Pondweed

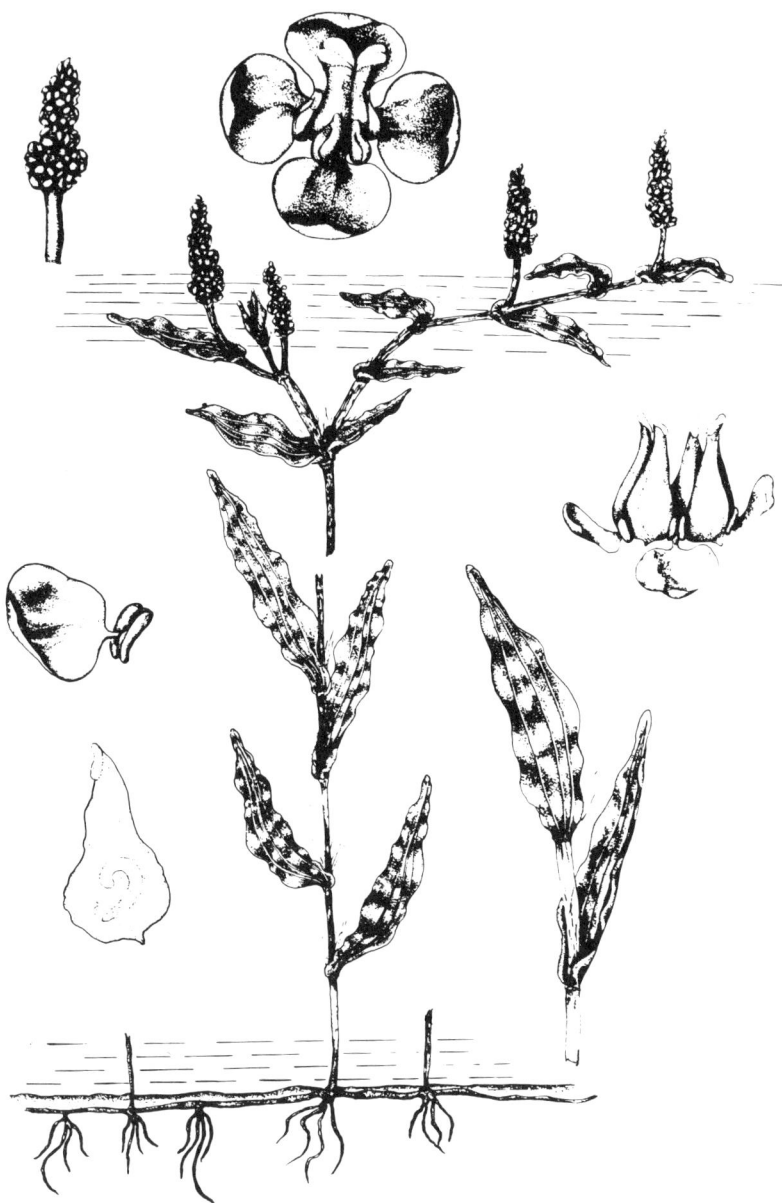

Clasping Leaved Pondweed

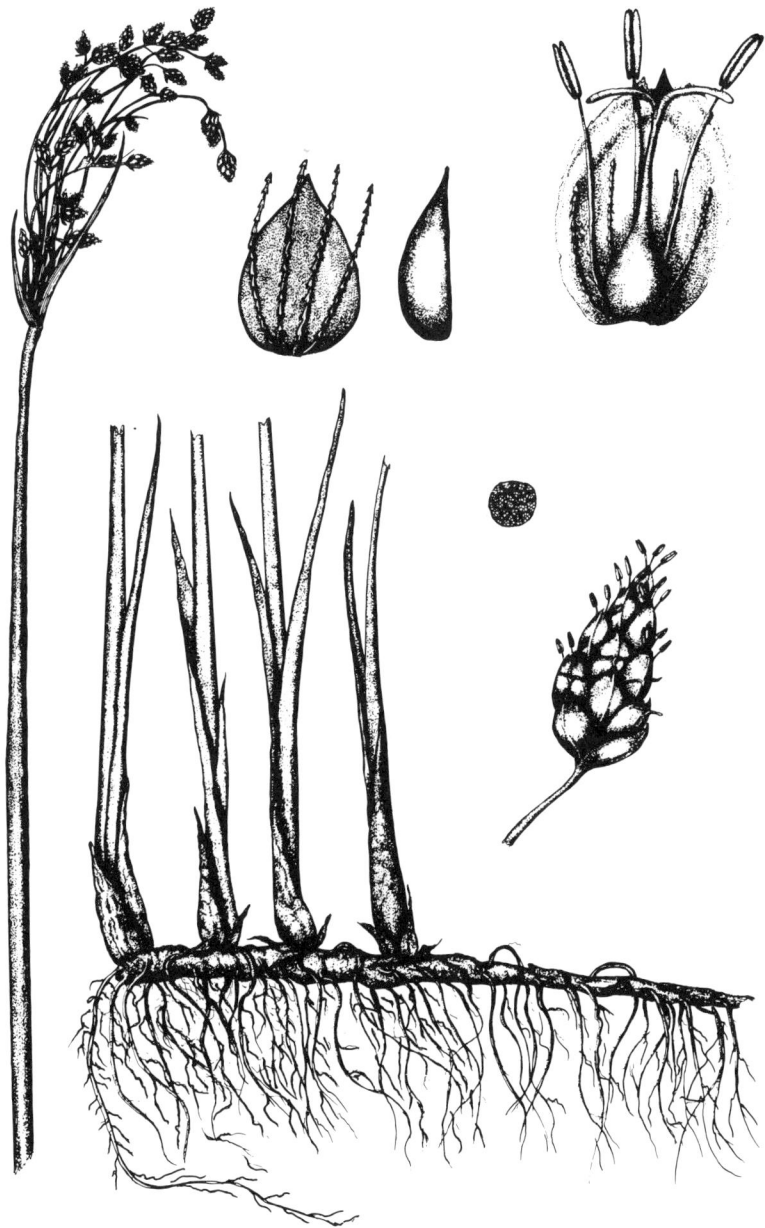

Great Bulrush

Sedges

Most of the nearly 200 species of sedges present have three-sided stems with three-ranked leaves. Often the leaves are finely toothed— or spiny—at the margin and on the lower midrib and can inflict severe cuts to arms and legs. These grasslike perennials generally inhabit wet meadows and swales, although a few grow best in standing water. One of these, creeping spike-rush (*Eleocharis palustris*), grows in shallow water at the margins of ponds, streams, and lakes. Such plants are objectionable at beaches because they hold organic debris that produces unpleasant odors when it decays.

Spike-rush resembles rushes in that its stems are nearly round and leafless—except at the base, where there is a red to brown sheath. The rootstocks are reddish and can produce a solid stand in a short time.

Duckweed

Duckweed is a common surface seed plant, often mistakenly identified as algae. There are three common species in the midwest: *Lemna minor* (common duckweed) and *L. trisulca* (star duckweed) and *Spirodela polyrhiza* (giant duckweed). All duckweed plants are at least 1/8 inch in size, whereas algae—such as water bloom and pond scum—are visible as individual plants only with the aid of a microscope. Thread-like algae and seaweed are larger, but do not resemble duckweeds.

Duckweeds have no organized leaf or stem tissue; only an undifferentiated plant body resembling a leaf, from which 1 root (in common duckweed), or 3 roots (in greater duckweed) hang down into the water.

Pond Scums and Water Bloom

Besides kelps and seaweeds, algae includes 2 other major types: the green pond scums, which are green-and- threadlike; and water bloom, which is made of bluish-green gelatinous balls. There are many useful and harmful species in each of these groups.

Water bloom generally include the blue-green algae. These algae are poisonous to animals (livestock, wild animals, birds, and pets) that drink water containing them. They also cause intestinal disorders in people—if present in water supplies—or if swimmers accidentally

Common Duckweed

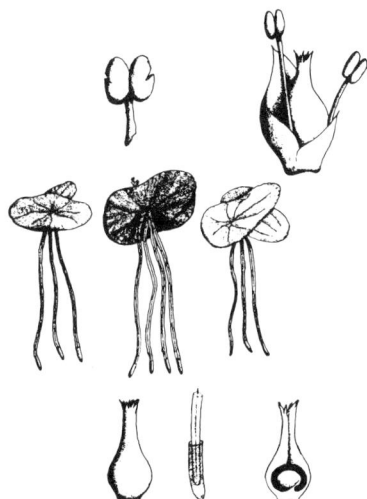

Greater Duckweed

Common Duckweed

Duckweed

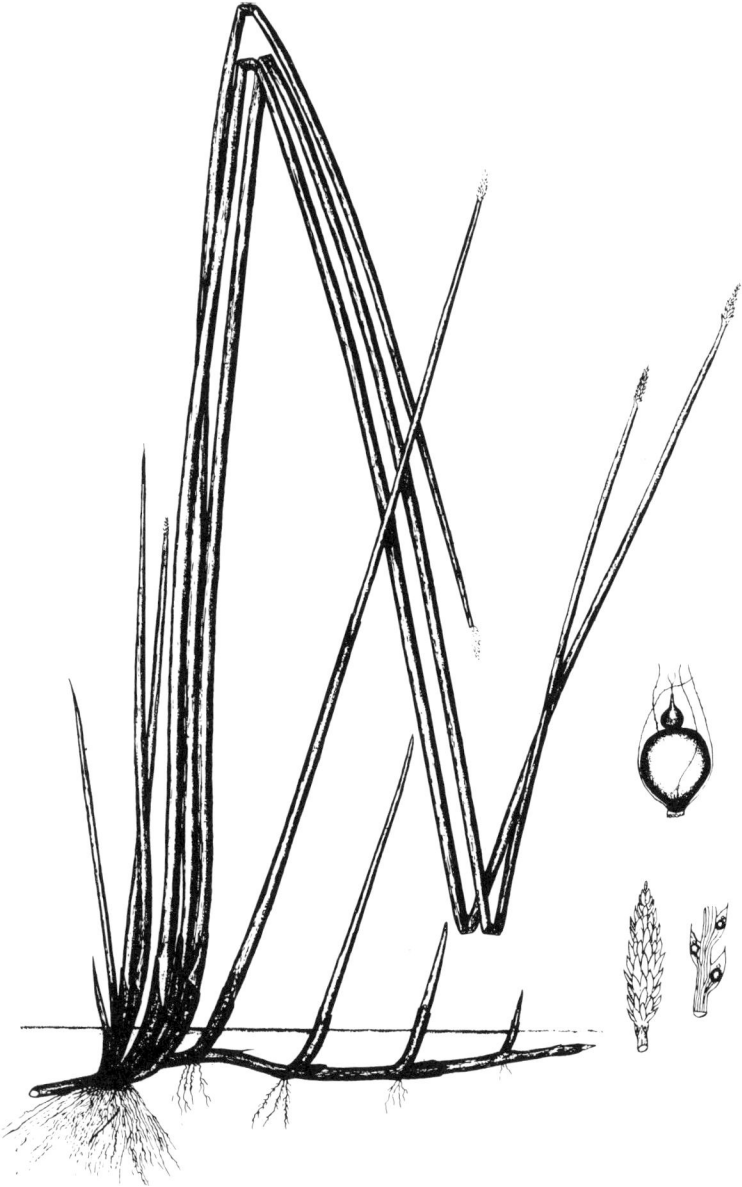

Creeping Spike-rush

drink the water. From swimming in water high in content of water bloom algae, some swimmers develop a skin rash. Blue-green algae impart a grassy odor to surface water if present in minute amounts: With an increase in amount, the odor becomes pungent. In high concentrations the odor is vile, resembling that of decaying fish. The odors from decaying water bloom algae and pond scums are most noticeable just before frost.

Scum-forming algae become noticeable in early summer, and increase in number up to September or October. They are especially common on the stagnant waters of ponds, lakes, and even some streams. Although they are a nuisance, they are not believed to be poisonous to animals that drink the water.

Control measures given in PESKY PLANTS are general. Specific herbicides are not included in this book, we suggest that you follow the recommendations on the label of the herbicide you use.

Control of Pesky Plants

Pesky plants usually can be controlled by one of these methods:

1. **Digging out.** This method usually is effective if few plants are involved. It may be impractical if plants are deep rooted or poisonous.

2. **Mowing.** If the area can be cleaned up and mowed regularly, most plants other than grasses and a few lawn weeds will not survive.

3. **Using herbicides** (weed control chemicals). Lists of some effective herbicides appear in other publications (see list below). Apply herbicides to the leaves and stems of plants or to the soil around them. Always read the labels and follow instructions carefully. You may kill desirable plants if you use herbicides improperly.

FOR MORE INFORMATION ON PLANTS THAT ARE PESKY, AND FOR SPECIFIC CONTROL MEASURES CHECK THE FOLLOWING PUBLICATIONS:

Aquatic Weed Control, Publications Mailing Room, 301 S. Second Street, Purdue University, LaFayette, IN 47905.

Controlling Canada Thistle, Ag. Bulletin, Rm. 245, 30 N. Murray St., University of Wisconsin, Madison, WI 53715.

Edible Wild Mushrooms, Distribution Center, 3 Coffey Hall, University of Minnesota, St. Paul, MN 55108.

Factors Affecting Foliar Applied Herbicides, Bulletin Office, P.O. Box 6640, Michigan State University, East Lansing, MI 48826-6640.

Grassy Weed Seedling Identification Key, Distribution Center, 3 Coffey Hall, University of Minnesota, St. Paul, MN 55108.

Growth Habits of Weeds, Distribution Center, 3 Coffey Hall, University of Minnesota, St. Paul, MN 55108.

Mushrooms and Other Related Fungi, Publications Distribution, Printing & Pub. Bldg., Iowa State University, Ames, IA 50011.

Noxious Weeds in Minnesota, Distribution Center, 3 Coffey Hall, University of Minnesota, St. Paul, MN 55108.

Plants Poisonous to Livestock, Distribution Center, 3 Coffey Hall, University of Minnesota, St. Paul, MN 55108.

Weeds of the North Central States, Distribution Center, 3 Coffey Hall, University of Minnesota, St. Paul, MN 55108.